Cambridge Elements

Elements in Public Policy
edited by
M. Ramesh
National University of Singapore (NUS)
Michael Howlett
Simon Fraser University, British Columbia
Xun WU
Hong Kong University of Science and Technology (Guangzhou)
Judith Clifton
University of Cantabria
Eduardo Araral
National University of Singapore (NUS)

BAD PUBLIC POLICY

Malignity, Volatility, and the Inherent Vices of Policy-Making

Michael Howlett
Simon Fraser University
Ching Leong
National University of Singapore
Tim Legrand
University of Adelaide

Shaftesbury Road, Cambridge CB2 8EA, United Kingdom

One Liberty Plaza, 20th Floor, New York, NY 10006, USA

477 Williamstown Road, Port Melbourne, VIC 3207, Australia

314–321, 3rd Floor, Plot 3, Splendor Forum, Jasola District Centre, New Delhi – 110025, India

103 Penang Road, #05–06/07, Visioncrest Commercial, Singapore 238467

Cambridge University Press is part of Cambridge University Press & Assessment, a department of the University of Cambridge.

We share the University's mission to contribute to society through the pursuit of education, learning and research at the highest international levels of excellence.

www.cambridge.org
Information on this title: www.cambridge.org/9781009497039

DOI: 10.1017/9781009497015

© Michael Howlett, Ching Leong and Tim Legrand 2025

This publication is in copyright. Subject to statutory exception and to the provisions of relevant collective licensing agreements, with the exception of the Creative Commons version the link for which is provided below, no reproduction of any part may take place without the written permission of Cambridge University Press & Assessment.

An online version of this work is published at doi.org/10.1017/9781009497015 under a Creative Commons Open Access license CC-BY-NC 4.0 which permits re-use, distribution and reproduction in any medium for non-commercial purposes providing appropriate credit to the original work is given and any changes made are indicated. To view a copy of this license visit https://creativecommons.org/licenses/by-nc/4.0

When citing this work, please include a reference to the DOI 10.1017/9781009497015

First published 2025

A catalogue record for this publication is available from the British Library

ISBN 978-1-009-49703-9 Hardback
ISBN 978-1-009-49702-2 Paperback
ISSN 2398-4058 (online)
ISSN 2514-3565 (print)

Cambridge University Press & Assessment has no responsibility for the persistence or accuracy of URLs for external or third-party internet websites referred to in this publication and does not guarantee that any content on such websites is, or will remain, accurate or appropriate.

Bad Public Policy

Malignity, Volatility, and the Inherent Vices of Policy-Making

Elements in Public Policy

DOI: 10.1017/9781009497015
First published online: April 2025

Michael Howlett
Simon Fraser University

Ching Leong
National University of Singapore

Tim Legrand
University of Adelaide

Author for correspondence: Michael Howlett, howlett@sfu.ca

Abstract: Policy studies assume the existence of baseline parameters – such as honest governments doing their best to create public value, publics responding in good faith, and both parties relying on a policy-making process that aligns with the public interest. In such circumstances, policy goals are expected to be produced through mechanisms in which the public can articulate its preferences and policy-makers are expected to listen to what has been said in determining their governments' courses of action. While these conditions are found in some governments, much policy-making occurs without these pre-conditions and processes. Unlike situations that produce what can be thought of as "good" public policy, "bad" public policy is a more common outcome. How this happens and what makes for bad public policy are the subjects of this Element. This title is also available as Open Access on Cambridge Core.

Keywords: policy process, policy failure, policy studies, policy design, risk management

© Michael Howlett, Ching Leong and Tim Legrand 2025

ISBNs: 9781009497039 (HB), 9781009497022 (PB), 9781009497015 (OC)
ISSNs: 2398-4058 (online), 2514-3565 (print)

Contents

1 Introduction   1

2 Studying the Darkside: Advancing the Concepts of Policy Risk, Malign Policy, and Policy Volatility in the Policy Sciences   9

3 The Darkside and the Brightside of Policy-Making: Democratic Values and the Policy Sciences   15

4 The Inherent Vices of Policy and Policy Design   33

5 A Risk Approach to the Management of Policy Volatility: Adverse Behavior and the Role of Procedural Policy Tools   44

6 Trends in the Management of Inherent Policy Volatility: Efforts to Manage Internal Policy Risk in Three OECD Countries   53

7 Conclusion: Vigilance and Vices   66

References   73

1 Introduction

Policy studies often simply assume the existence of baseline parameters which facilitate the development of "good" policies, such as honest governments doing their best to create public value, publics responding in good faith and fair dealing, and both parties relying on policy-making processes that align squarely with the public interest (Moore, 1995; 2014). That is, ones which enjoy popular support and expert consensus and which are dedicated to enhancing public welfare. In such circumstances "good" policies are commonly expected to be produced through open mechanisms and participatory procedures in which the public can articulate its preferences and policy-makers listen to, and act in good faith upon, what has been said in determining their governments' courses of action (Howlett, 2020).

While these conditions and processes are indeed found in some circumstances in liberal democratic governments, in practice there is ample evidence from around the world, and even there, that much policy-making occurs without these pre-conditions and processes in place (Legrand & Jarvis, 2014; McConnell, 2018; Jarvis & Legrand, 2018). In such circumstances "bad" public policy is a more common outcome: that is, policies which reflect only very partial knowledge, are enacted at the behest of special interests or with decision-maker self-enrichment in mind, and typically fail to promote the social good. Exactly how this happens and what it is that makes for "bad" public policy are the subjects of this Element.

One concern, for example, which is somewhat independent of regime type, is maliciousness or the use of policy-making machinery to punish opposition or groups and individuals deemed undesirable. If the ethical basis of good public policy is concerned with its *alignment* with beneficial principles of public value and a latent concern for prioritizing the public interest, it can be considered *malign* where it is not.

Attention to these kinds of "negative" policy dynamics is the concern of what we describe as the emerging study of the "darkside" of public policy: where the consequences of factors such as uncertainty, malign (and relatedly, misaligned) policies, poor compliance, and other factors such as a lack of preparation in the face of new or existing challenges and problems, and a failure to learn from past experiences produce, at best, ineffective or inefficient outcomes (Howlett, 2020; 2022). At worst, such policies can marginalize, exclude, and funnel state resources away from vulnerable sections of the public or replace the public interest with private rent-seeking behavior in ways that intentionally evade the public interest and create little or no public value, or even detract from it (Moore, 1994; Wintrobe, 2000; Leong & Howlett, 2022).

This Element aims to conceptualize and theorize this topic in the context of policy studies and the growing interest in policy design (Howlett, 2024). It argues that better understanding and planning for this "darkside" of policy-making is of growing urgency and importance in studies of policy-making and is a necessary adjunct to most studies of policy design, which tend to live on the "brightside" of policy-making (Douglas et al., 2021). It deals with how best to conceptualize and deal with the phenomena of bad policy, including maliciousness and internal risks of malfeasance but also looking at non-compliance and other similar "inherent vices" or internal risks of policy-making.

Although these kinds of problems are often acknowledged as common occurrences in policy-making processes, they have rarely been studied systematically in the policy sciences (Goodin, 1980; Leong & Howlett, 2022). This Element draws on the previous work of the three co-authors who have studied these phenomena for several years and produced a record of published work detailing this darkside, exploring how it leads to policy failures and poor design processes and discussing how bad policy occurs and how it can be corrected (Legrand, 2022). It summarizes, synthesizes, and condenses this work to provide a definitive short study of the subject.

Defining the Darkside

Although a distinct wave of "post-positivist," critical and/or interpretivist scholarship emerged in the last two decades of the 20th century which engaged with the role of values, beliefs, and politics in decision-making, policy thinking from its origins has continuously been criticized for its overly optimistic and often technocratic or 'positivist' tenor and its general neglect of many of the practical problems of policy-making (Tribe, 1972).

The "darkside" of public policy discussed in this Element is metaphorical in two senses: it refers both to the opacity of decision-making processes and to the "dark" or less than public interested motives of many of those involved in policy-making and "policy taking." As such, it can be contrasted with the "brightside" of policy-making and policy studies that deal with less self-interested and more transparent processes and outcomes (Compton et al., 2019; Douglas et al., 2021).

Problems with policy designs caused by the darkside of policy-making – the uncertainty inherent to real-world political settings, as well as the endemic recalcitrance of many policy-makers and policy-takers to comply with or promote the public interest and public value in their activities – remain very much underexplored in the orthodox policy studies literature (Colebatch, 2018; Turnbull, 2018; Howlett, 2020). The larger thrust of research in policy sciences and adjacent literatures remains firmly oriented toward the production of modelling and generalizable insights that accrue from a dispassionate, scientific engagement with policy-making, which is held as a process that is expected to deliver on government goals, and to do so in an efficient way (see Farr, Hacker & Kazee, 2006; Durnová & Weible, 2020).

This literature on policy-making and policy design, while well-disposed to help deal with many "external" crises and changes that pose risks to government goal attainment, has examined much less thoroughly the behavior of policy-makers and policy takers (Howlett et al., 2020), which pose "inherent" risks to good policy outcomes. These risks are linked to the nature and logic of policy-making itself and whether and how it is carried out in the public interest.

It is only fairly recently that the literature on policy design and practice has recognized the importance of identifying and accounting for this kind of "risk" (Howlett et al., 2022). However, other policy-related literatures, especially those that fall under or overlap with political science, law and public administration, have long-accepted that the ideal of good government is continually besieged by a range of pathologies and manipulative practices (Goodin, 1980). These works variously include explanations of how badly construed information can skew government policy, especially where state and governance knowledge bases and capacities are limited; how decision-making are often motivated by interests other than the creation of public value; and how policy targets – those whose behaviors government attempts to manage – often embark on forms of lawful and unlawful "misconduct," such as fraud, gamesmanship, evasion, deliberate non-compliance, and others, to undermine government intentions (Saward, 1992; Howlett, 2020).

This tendency toward optimism is understandable for several reasons. First, much policy and policy-making "on the darkside" is almost by definition opaque and resistant to scrutiny and analysis. This is the case, for example, with corruption or covert practices, which agents involved in them often try to cover-up and with the malign exercise of power in the interests of national security, for example, which states generally make opaque, do not publicize and protect with preventative information disclosure laws. It is also the case with corporate and special interest groups lobbying policy-makers to protect their private interests, which have in the past resulted in harms to the public interest including, variously, environmental contamination, tropical rainforest deforestation, smoking, alcohol consumption, licit and illicit drug use, and beyond. Obscuring these kinds of influence, as well as the outcomes, is very much part of the malignity of such influencers (Oreskes & Conway, 2011).

Many policy scientists do widely declaim such lack of inclusion and transparency as indicators of poor policy-making practice, but a more fundamental value is also at stake in this behavior: the essence of democracy or rule of the people which demands that the public be able to properly evaluate government performance and reward or punish them in elections for incompetence, corruption, or other kinds of policy and political scandals and failures.

Diamond and Morlino, for example, specify the minimum qualities of democracy are "1) universal, adult suffrage; 2) recurring, free, competitive, and fair elections; 3) more than one serious political party; and 4) alternative sources of information" (2004, p. 21). The latter point is often overlooked, but it is in fact pivotal. To assess whether their interests are well-served, the public must have ample high-quality and accurate information on government efforts, intents, and outcomes. The principle of transparency is often expected to be provided by a free, untrammeled press corps and through access to government information, but in practice often neither function effectively in this manner. In reality, the conglomeration of media ownership and broad exemptions to freedom of information laws mean that even in liberal-democratic regimes many government intentions and outcomes can remain hidden in the shadows. As Hallsworth and Rutter (2011) note, "The more that this process is illusory, the more democracy is undermined."

Second, bad policy is by definition non-inclusive. The exclusion of specific sections of the public, either selectively or entirely, from participating in policy-creation processes and outcomes can be, and often is, the result of poor practice or unconscious bias, but is also often the result of *intentional* structural and agential strategies to shape how policy is made, and whom it benefits. Rather than promote openness and transparency, these efforts can intentionally exclude, occlude, preclude, or ostracize some sections of the populace in order to meet nefarious and undemocratic goals, from overly rewarding loyal or client-groups to exchanges of favors with campaign financiers or the personal enrichment of civil servants or politicians, or worse (Herzog, 2018).

Third, many purportedly beneficial policies in practice rely on expected and anticipated high levels of compliance of those targeted by policies with government aims (Weaver, 2015). This includes mundane activities such as having members of the public generally obey traffic laws and pay their taxes, but also expecting contractors and service providers to comply with contract terms and intentions or individuals not gaming rules and regulations or otherwise failing to comply with their intent. Although often assumed to be automatic, compliance behaviors almost always require compliance mechanisms of monitoring, enforcement, and sanctions, which come with sometimes large additional costs (Weaver, 2009). These compliance efforts often do not themselves perform well and thus limit the reach and effectiveness of the policy. Uncertain compliance and policing thus introduce additional risks into policy-making that lead to uncertain outcomes, even with the best of intentions (Weaver, 2013).

Phenomena such as non-compliance and self-interested or malign policy behavior are termed here "*policy vices*" and, importantly, can occur in all different kinds of states and at all different levels within them. While more prevalent in forms of government less concerned with the public interest than democratic states, they also occur in liberal democratic ones, although the ethics of open government, participation, and probity associated with democratic states are expected to limit the opportunities for such behavior and resulting bad policy to emerge (Legrand, 2021). Additionally, such vices can come from all segments of civil society and public life, not just governmental actors.

Beyond Capacity Challenges: The Idea of Inherent Policy Vices

Previous studies, of course, have noted that policies do not always succeed (McConnell, 2010). But these studies have often argued that poor policy-making and policy outcomes are not inherent to the policy process but rather often emerge from capacity limits in the face of external challenges: so that, for example, poorly paid civil servants in many poor countries may have little option but recourse to bribes and favoritism in order to survive in their positions (Graycar, 2013, 2015) or that better analysis and more administrative resources can ensure better policy formulation and implementation of government plans (Ingram & Schneider, 1990; Cameron & Evans, 2024).

But while this may be true in some instances, one key pillar of our thesis is that the challenges facing the achievement of better policy outputs and outcomes amount to more than simply overcoming capacity limits and external risks. While it is true that some of the problems encountered by policy-makers and policy thinkers are indeed due to a mismatch between the external and internal funding demands and other environmental challenges faced by government, and that often critical capacity challenges do exist (Howlett & Ramesh, 2016), it is the argument of this Element that there are other additional risks that are *inherent* to policy-making and cannot be avoided, although they can be mitigated.

These risks to policy-making can be framed as sources of *policy volatility* or the likelihood or propensity of any policy design to fail. Like a stock portfolio in which some failures are expected and can be hedged against, it is argued here that policy designs must deal with these kinds of internal risks head-on rather than simply assume that all will simply work out for the best if a government's intentions are good (Howlett & Leong, 2022).

Howlett and Leong (2022), for example, have pointed to the importance of three such *inherent vices* or risks to public policy, which are detailed in subsequent sections. These include the inherent uncertainty of policy-making, as well as malice on the part of policy-makers and non-compliance in policy-takers, as set out earlier. Together with other problems such as (un)preparedness and (non)learning identified by other authors (Dunlop, 2017; McConnell, 2002), the omnipresence of these vices challenges many aspects of contemporary policy theory that were developed in earlier periods when these kinds of vices or risks were largely ignored or simply assumed away.

Thus, as Legrand (2021) has argued, many current problems in policy theory and practice are now often seen to be the product of a crisis in the core values that previously defined the telos of "the good state" – commonly viewed as a benign representative public body designed to enhance public values in a relatively unproblematic way. In this view the main impediment to the achievement of the public interest has often been posited to be inadequate knowledge of exactly how to identify the public interest or interests, or a lack of the resources needed to pursue or achieve such interests, rather than being due to the nature of the task itself or to the characteristics of the principal actors who define, address and take part in it (Moore, 1995; 2014; Colebatch, 2010).

Recent examples such as the "war on terror" post-9-11, the 2008 financial crises, and the 2019 COVID pandemic show that global challenges can trigger societal polarization and generate crises for the rule of law, upsetting the balance of support for state action and leading to declining trust in institutions. All of these have extensive implications for the quality of democracy and government. Bennett and Lemoine (2014a), for example, are only two of many observers of what is often thought to be an increase in such phenomena, noting many trends toward increased volatility, uncertainty, and complexity in world affairs and arguing they only promise to increase in future years as wars and climate change impacts increase in an ever more highly interconnected world. They term this policy environment as one that is increasingly volatile, uncertain, complex, and ambiguous (VUCA).

We argue here, however, that these developments have not so much introduced new elements into policy-making but have rather exacerbated problems already *inherent* to policy-making itself. Extensive regulatory capture, especially by powerful firms; the normalization of policy goals that transgress human rights; and deliberate obfuscation of the policy process by its core players in many countries for security purposes, or by leaders who lambast the media and engage in corrupt and venal practices, have always posed a threat to traditional notions of effective policy-making in the public interest, even where this latter sentiment was common. In other countries where open and transparent government has never been the norm, already sizable problems with these modes and ways of thinking have intensified even further.

This adds a new dimension to the idea of a "darkside" of policy-making as not only a perennial problem but a worsening one and lends urgency to efforts to better understand these policy risks and mitigate them. These flaws and vices have been with us for some time, but they flourish in volatile policy environments, and amid the "dark" misalignment of the public interest and policy settings in many countries it must be asked what are the prospects for policy studies to help resolve these challenges (Peters and Nagel, 2025). These considerations motivate this volume.

Aim of the Element

To further this end, this Element develops terms and concepts such as policy volatility, policy malignancy, and policy vices not as a wholly new platform for research, but rather as a means to marshal the existing range of theoretical and conceptual work on these aspects of policy-making. Recognition of how these pathologies carry over into policy-making currently remains limited in the policy literature (Arestis & Kitromilides, 2010; Legrand, 2022) and correcting this gap is a major aim of this Element.

Specifically, the Element draws from recent work in policy studies that focusses attention to these kinds of behaviors in much the same way as, for example, Allan McConnell does in dealing with "hidden agendas" or policies with covert aims lurking behind ostensible purposes (McConnell, 2018). It further examines the question of how policy scholars should engage with long-standing internal risks amidst a decline in the normative democratic principles of good governance that were presumed in earlier eras (Wagle, 2000) and discusses what lessons can be derived from current and past studies for improving policy practice in such an environment.

Structure of the Element

This opening section makes the case for the need for policy-makers to pay attention to the darkside of policy-making and more closely examine their own behavior and that of policy targets in formulating and implementing policies and undertaking their design. It introduced key concepts to be used in the analysis from "policy volatility" to "inherent vices," which are useful in this endeavor.

Section 2 then surveys emerging policy theory, concepts, and research on the "darkside" of policy-making, sketching out a framework of analysis that accommodates multidisciplinary contributions to better understanding these topics. The foundation of this framework is normative, insofar as it appeals to principles of non-subjugation, public service ethos, and universal human rights, and it seeks to advance effective and legitimate policy-making behaviors by understanding their limits and constraints. It explains how the use of utilitarian measures and hedonic compliance-deterrence models in the policy sciences has dominated the field and contributed to some of the problems encountered in identifying and correcting internal policy risks. By bringing together conceptual possibilities and normative values in this framework, the section establishes a theoretical beachhead for better understanding and managing the "darkside" of public policy. The section argues for the need to re-examine policy-making problems and limits in order to address their presence in policy-making, as well as for a better recognition of what greater uncertainty implies for the likelihood of policy success and failure and the reasons for them.

Section 3 then offers a normative critique of the traditional policy studies literature and examines in detail the general notion of malign or "bad" policy. As this introduction has pointed out, the disciplinary development of policy studies has long been shaped by scholars working within liberal democratic traditions. In consequence, a long-held assumption has been that policy-making is, *prima facie*, motivated exclusively by the pursuit of the public interest, and this assumption has gone largely unchallenged, even while intersecting critical traditions – particularly in political science – have opened up rich research agendas on topics such as historical bias and institutional and agential harms (Goodin, 1980). The section critiques the often-latent assumptions of benevolence found in many policy studies and develops the notion of political exclusion as a methodological means to identify deviations from liberal democracy's precepts.

Section 4 then expands on five specific categories of inherent vices associated with volatility in policy-making set out earlier: namely uncertainty, maliciousness, (non)compliance; unpreparedness and non-learning, with a focus on the lesser-explored first three. Exploring the origins and development of these problems the section suggests ways to mitigate and address the contributions that these vices make to the darkside of public policy.

Section 5 discusses how, precisely, proposed policies can be assessed and altered to promote and lead to more benevolent outcomes. It shows how each of the risks set out in earlier sections can be managed through a variety of means from institutionalizing foresight agencies in order to deal with the risk of surprises affecting government agendas, in the case of unpreparedness, to the implementation of mandated and comprehensive evaluation and measurement activities in order to reduce the risk of poor or non-learning in policy evaluation. The section emphasizes the kinds of "procedural" tools or techniques governments have at their disposal to deal with these vices (Howlett, 2000). These are tools (Bali et al., 2021) that are put into place to control aspects of policy processes and policy behaviors rather than, as in the case of more substantive tools such as a public enterprise or regulatory commission, to alter the behavior of actors involved in delivering specific kinds of goods and services in society.

Section 6 continues this discussion and draws on a comparative analysis of recent empirical experiences in several OECD countries attempting to address these inherent risks and concerns. The section sets out a set of management practices that can help inform policy design and curb the worst excesses of bad policy.

Finally, we conclude **Section 7** with a call to make malignity, volatility, and inherent vices mainstream concepts in policy analysis. Our concern in this Element is not just that these are real and corrosive phenomena but that they have gone unnoticed or sidelined by all but a handful of policy scholars. If good policy-making is, at heart, a result of a shared normative commitment to values of transparency and openness and the public good, then safeguarding that commitment requires ongoing vigilance and mitigation. It is our plea for such vigilance from the policy science community that concludes the Element.

2 Studying the Darkside: Advancing the Concepts of Policy Risk, Malign Policy, and Policy Volatility in the Policy Sciences

Introduction: Dr. Pangloss and the Policy Sciences

Is all for the best, in the best of all possible worlds? Voltaire's 1759 satirical work *Candide; or The Optimist*, tells the story of the eponymous hero and his mentor Professor Pangloss who is always prone to see even the worst possible circumstance as part of God's beneficial plan for humanity. Candide is taught in his early years living in a garden of paradise the Leibnitzian philosophy that, "all is for the best in the best of all possible worlds." The story follows Candide as he leaves his garden idyll and encounters the outside world, and despite seeing a world of apparent violence, tragedy, and suffering, tries to maintain his unfaltering, but increasingly ludicrous optimism in the face of the realities of a very uncertain and unhelpful present.

Voltaire's novel is satirical, but for contemporary policy studies there are instructive parallels. Not so long ago, a widespread view about the nature of the world in the post-Cold War period, for example, held that liberal democracy represented a kind of ideological gravity well that peoples of the world would be inevitably drawn toward as the best of all possible worlds unfolded in the absence of a totalitarian threat. Francis Fukuyama's teleological "end of history" analysis was the apotheosis of this view, heralding liberal democracy's ideological supremacy and inevitability. For much of the world, he argued, "there is now no ideology with pretensions to universality that is in a position to challenge liberal democracy, and no universal principle of legitimacy other than the sovereignty of the people," thus anticipating a gradual, but still fairly rapid, movement toward utopia (Fukuyama, 1992).

Yet subsequent global trends in illiberal, autocratic and poor government and governance have revealed that we are not at the end of history, and there is mounting evidence of a continued malaise in many formerly prominent liberal democratic regimes across the world that are under attack from populism and a distinct trend toward authoritarianism (Howlett, 2021; Legrand, 2021).

Now more than ever, policy-makers and scholars in more and more countries alike must deal directly, and with eyes wide open, with the "darkside" of policy-making. Many of these aspects of policy-making are unavoidable, being part of the "inherent vices" of the subject in the same way that food will spoil and ships will sink. These kinds of behaviors have always been with us but are arguably more pronounced and/or take a different shape in the present-day interconnected, social media saturated, and increasingly volatile, uncertain, complex, and ambiguous world.

This section examines key concepts in the field that allow us to better understand these phenomena and the risks they pose to "good" policy-making.

Dealing with a Messy Policy World

Understanding the risks posed to policy-making can be framed as understanding the sources of *policy volatility* or the likelihood or propensity of any given policy design to fail. Howlett and Leong argue that policy designs must deal with such volatility head-on rather than assume simply that all will work out well in the best of all possible worlds (Howlett & Leong, 2022). Legrand, similarly, has argued that many current problems in much existing policy theory and practice are caused by a crisis in the core values of liberal democracy that underlie much of the policy sciences. That is, that the values and freedoms that previously defined the telos of "the good state" toward which all policies were commonly thought to be oriented, or at least should be oriented toward if they are to be beneficial and serve the public interest, are difficult to maintain and are not an automatic or default condition.

That having been said, in the current era, policy problems are more interwoven and their solutions often more ambiguous than in previous years, often with an interlocking international and national dimension which can make them more intractable (Levin et al., 2014). But the challenges facing policy-makers are more than simply an administrative or political system capacity challenge. Cousins (2018), for example, has identified the volatile, uncertain, complex, and ambiguous (VUCA) nature of the world as the central characteristic of the current policy environment that has serious continuing consequences for effective public policy-making and policy designs.

Legrand (2022), for example, has argued that much of the current crisis in liberal democratic countries was provoked in part by post-2001 anti-terrorism measures which, among other things, ushered into liberal democratic regimes many aspects of a surveillance state that are incompatible with pre-existing liberal freedoms of movement, speech, and due process, and in part by the financial collapse of 2007–2008, which laid bare wealth inequality, undermining belief in equality of opportunity and of the legitimacy of liberal economies and societies. The challenges posed to nation states, especially in the Middle East and Europe, by immigration and refugee flows resulting from the Post-Arab Spring era and rise of the Islamic State in Iraq and Syria, also fed ethnic tensions and illiberal nationalistic reactions.

As a result of these overlapping set of events, many democracies are now experiencing problems linked to an erosion of the rule of law and declining trust in institutions and have been unable to avoid the normalization of policy goals that transgress previous concerns for expanding human rights. Deliberate obfuscation of the policy process by core players in many countries who pass laws against press freedom, subvert elections, and engage in corrupt and venal practices in government has proliferated in such contexts. This all amounts to growth in the "darkside" of policy-making, a side of policy-making that citizens and policy-makers must be alert to and not discount or minimize.

As highlighted in Section 1, Howlett and Leong (2023) and others have suggested many of these problems encountered if not promoted by policy-makers and policy thinkers in the present era are not new but have always been with us and can be considered *inherent vices* or inevitable risks to public policy. These include problems linked to the inherent uncertainty of policy-making, often the presence of malice in policy-makers and that of non-compliance in policy-takers, as well as problems related to a lack of preparation for surprises and an all-too-common inability to learn from past experience.

It is reasonable to ask how the tenets of the policy sciences are capable of dealing with this reality in its present manifestation and to what extent Panglossian thinking about policy-making is able to deal with the decidedly non-Panglossian reality of contemporary world affairs. The origins and impacts of these problems are discussed in more depth in Section 3, but suffice it to say that together these problems challenge many aspects of contemporary policy theory and design practice even at the best of times (Peters and Nagel 2025).

The Emergence of a Panglossian Vision in Contemporary Policy Studies

Our contention is that scholars of the policy sciences need to take this "darkside" at least as seriously as the "brightside" and think more carefully and clearly about how to move forward policies capable of dealing with both these directions in society and public affairs. Many contemporary policy studies often cling to a more Panglossian view of the health of democratic and other governmental systems which, as with Voltaire's hero, leads to actions and plans that fail in the face of change and adverse behavior (Howlett, 2021).

Just as Candide critiques the naivety of philosophers who saw the world as one of a "pre-established harmony," policy designs that take such values as free expression as given and consider policy-making to be a *fait accompli* in which policy-makers and policy-takers are assumed to always operate in good faith to advance the public interest are, on our view, problematic. Any work that is confined to only sharpening policy delivery – producing cost efficient and effective goal fulfilment – while remaining blind to the normative questions of whether policy goals align with precepts of public value, or are misappropriated to serve marginal interests, are ignored or malevolently exploited – is equally so. It is imperative to question whether policy-makers and policy takers do, in fact, always operate in good faith, and to understand when and why this occurs. This need has never been more pressing, nor more central to the discipline.

The Policy Orientation Then and Now

It was not always thus. Lasswell's vision of a liberal policy science seventy-five years ago was forged in response to the abhorrent "darkside" of policy-making that had manifested itself clearly in 1920s, 1930s, and 1940s Europe (Torgerson, 2024). The "policy orientation" Lasswell espoused was a reaction to, and rose against, an earlier era of Panglossian Wilsonian thinking in the immediate post-WWI era, which drove some of that later behavior (Lasswell, 1951).

Lasswell and his contemporaries deplored the malign consequences of the ruthless, secret, and unaccountable bureaucratic machinery found in authoritarian and totalitarian states, and the apparent ease with which many ostensibly democratic states around the world had acquiesced to the malign values of Nazi, fascist, and military regimes. They set about advocating for a "policy sciences of democracy," a field oriented normatively toward the nurturing and strengthening of democracy and human dignity. The aim, Lasswell argued, was to avoid the emergence of a "garrison state" dominated by security elites, and to place "civilian supremacy" at its center, through which civil liberties, freedom of information, and equality were to be assured (Lasswell, 1950, pp. 57–58). Lasswell's outlook was, and remains, an essentially liberal democratic vision for academics concerned with beneficial public policy-making, while recognizing full well the possible presence of alternative and less-altruistic forms of government and policy behavior and the need for vigilence if such alternatives were to be defeated.

Thus for the early generation of policy scientists writing in the 1950s and early 1960s, the challenge was to resurrect the brightside, in a more pragmatic way, from its turn-of-the-century progressive progenitor and prove that governments, and especially liberal democracies, could function at least as well, if not much better, than their authoritarian and totalitarian counterparts. In the wake of a hard-fought victory over authoritarian and totalizing governments in Europe and Asia, harnessing an axiomatic belief in the supremacy of the liberal democratic tradition was thought to be the means to achieve "congruence between the preferences of citizens and the actions of policy-makers" throughout the world as a new cold war got underway (Huber & Powell, 1994).

This made a great deal of sense in the post-war epoch and educating a new cadre of scholars – the "policy scientists of democracy" – was rightfully thought to be a means through which this new generation could act as the architects and engineers of the new beneficial system, building institutions that could withstand any further attempt to establish "garrison states" bent to the whims of narrow ideological elites (Lasswell, 1971).

Seventy-five years later, such imperatives have waned, and the misalignment of democratic policy principles and the many policy goals pursued by governments around the world has in many cases reversed the onus of this optimistic vision of the policy sciences. Many politicians and members of the public for example, now deplore efforts made to promote evidence-based policy-making as elitist, while similarly condemning any effort to harness greater levels of expertise to the service of the public. This is true of many developed countries currently in the thrall of populist movements although, somewhat paradoxically, in other areas of the world, where colonialism, political instability, and poor economic conditions prevented the early adoption of more Panglossian attitudes, that vision remains fresh and increasing efforts are being made to create and educate a corps of policy scientists imbued with it in many countries in Asia, Africa, and Latin America (Brik & Pal, 2021, St. Denny & Zittoun, 2024).

Continuing to work as if the current world only needs more democracy or participation in order to undo would-be tyrants or develop effective policy, however, is dangerous. This is amply illustrated by the 1990s blockbuster, Jurassic Park, which tells a morality tale akin to Voltaire's idyll-turned-cataclysm. The film's story centers on a theme park set in an island paradise repopulated by dinosaurs from the benign Brachiosaurus to the dangerous Tyrannosaurus Rex, all made possible by the remarkable scientific feat of creating genetic clones of dinosaurs drawn from ancient DNA preserved in amber. In a terse exchange on the dangers of this project with the park's billionaire creator, the realist Dr Ian Malcom remarks: "Yeah, yeah, but your scientists were so preoccupied with whether they could, they didn't stop to think if they should." The ensuing catastrophic failure of the park's security has disastrous consequences for all, which the park's Panglossian creators are helpless to contain. An unleashed T. Rex – literally, "King of the Tyrant Lizards" – wreaks untold destruction before the story's heroes manage their escape. There is little ambiguity in the movie's moral caution concerning the consequences of the pursuit of actions without a clear sense of the consequences of what could go wrong and a much better appreciation of the risks of not only known but also the unknown consequences of these pursuits.

This is not the first time this kind of critique of an essentially Panglossian technocratic vision of policy-making has been made (Fischer, 1990). In 1985 Lawrence Mead, for example, spoke of how policy sciences' adherence to economics both in spirit and methodology – a discipline that "tended to serve interests indiscriminately" – had outweighed its original Lasswellian political or ethical pluralism and led to an overly optimistic or naïve policy science whereby policies were discussed only in terms of costs and benefits, incentive or disincentives (Mead, 1985). And as with Jurassic Park's catastrophic conclusion, such efforts to create an ethics-free policy science can give rise to, and serve, dangerous forces just as easily as more just or benign ones.

Conclusion: The Role of the Policy Sciences in a Changing World

Any Panglossian adaptation of the original "policy orientation," as Lasswell termed it, is problematic for several reasons (Torgerson, 2024). One problem is the view that a policy science, like the public administration system of old, can be a neutral technocratic exercise marshalling evidence about "what works, when" and should have little or no role to play in the setting of policy goals (as Wilson [1887] argued in an earlier era in the case of the emerging field of public administration). Goals, in this strict separationist view, are defined as "political" and beyond the purview of analysts whose normative aim should only be to improve the efficiency of goal implementation.

This is a problem of "commission." But there are also problems of "omission," a concern that is more analytical in nature as the process of exacting generalizable insights in the development of a policy science is often confined to looking at the system in aggregate or structural terms rather than behavioral ones (Dryzek, 2002). The central goal of policy inquiry, indeed, was sometimes seen to be to develop model processes and system in which individuals – policymakers and policy takers – are simply assumed to play by the rules. But this is to live in the Panglossian world highlighted earlier rather than examine in detail actual policy behavior, which should be the true expectation of a real policy science (Stokey & Zeckhauser, 1978; Leong and Howlett, 2020; Howlett and Leong, 2022).

As shall be argued in the sections which follow, policy design is fundamentally flawed when it does not align with the delivery of public value, when it fails to learn the lessons of the past, or when it assumes a level of certainty which does not exist, failing to prepare for obvious and less obvious eventualities and depends for its success only upon the goodwill of the policy-maker and/or policy taker (van Buuren et al., 2023). Rather, the role of policy science is to find ways to design institutions and processes that enable learning and preparation, reduce uncertainty and lead to the transparent articulation of public interests irrespective of, indeed, in anticipation of, precisely the (lack-of) goodwill and commitment to those values on the part of policy-makers and -takers (Hirschman, 1977).

3 The Darkside and the Brightside of Policy-Making: Democratic Values and the Policy Sciences

It is axiomatic in much of the policy sciences that policy-making should align with what are essentially liberal democratic principles. As mentioned in the previous section, in this view policy goals are expected to be produced through open and participatory procedures in which the public can articulate its preferences to policy-makers while policy-makers are expected to listen to what has been said in public forums in determining their governments' courses of action. Public policy is *public* then, insofar as its mandate for action derives from the public's expression of will in an election, and it is *policy* insofar as it marshals the resources of the state (from taxation, assets, and so on) via its institutions to realize that mandate.

Of course many states have autocratic, dictatorial, or other kinds of states in which these democratic processes and fora do not exist and discussion of open and participatory procedures is moot or remains aspirational at best (Wintrobe, 1998). But this ideal typical model of policy-making also does not occur all the time even in liberal democratic states. Precisely why this is the case is a subject that requires careful analysis.

In the following two sections we develop two concepts introduced in earlier sections that help to describe and explain why this model fails to occur even in many instances in liberal democratic states: "policy volatility" – the propensity of policies to fail – and the idea of "inherent vices" or the notion that some sources or risks of failure are inevitable and can be at best mitigated and never eliminated. In this section the role of normative values in public policy-making is discussed while the inherent vices of policy-making, policy volatility, and their design implications are the subject of discussion in Section 4.

Introduction: Normative Values and Policy-Making

The question of whether and how policy scholars should engage with normative democratic principles continues to divide the policy sciences (see Wagle, 2000, for an excellent exposition). Understanding the origins and impact of the trends set out earlier is made difficult not only by the optimistic world view of many in the field but also by the tendency of this view to be exacerbated by the nature of the contemporary scholar-practitioner relationships. Much scholarship follows the funding set out for it by non-disinterested governments, NGOs, foundations, and private companies (Oreskes & Conway, 2011), and increasingly, the scholar-practitioner relationship in the policy sciences and related fields is one in which government agencies act as agenda-setters and research-takers. As a result, the discipline now flirts with a form of capture whereby "relevance" or use by practitioners is ranked highly and the scope of policy research is determined and its validity rubber-stamped (or not) by the subjects of the research itself – usually government (Jarvis & Howlett, 2021).

This makes investigations of the darkside of policy-making less likely and less prevalent than one would think. But it is also true that the "darkside" outlined in the previous section is a difficult concept to investigate for other reasons. Here it should be recalled that the concept of the "darkside" is metaphorical in two senses: it refers, on the one hand, to the opacity of decision-making processes that makes their analysis and theorization difficult and often inferential and, on the other, to the sometimes malign motives of those responsible for developing policies and implementing decisions which are hidden or difficult to discern. Policy-making is often opaque at the best of times while in many situations – such as those surrounding corruption or malfeasance – efforts are often made by participants to conceal their actions.

Nevertheless, there are some actions that clearly signal malign or malicious intent. Moves to make a policy process *less* transparent, for example, are often telltale signs of non-Panglossian intent while the exclusion of the public, selectively or blanket, from participation in a policy is another non-Panglossian "tell." In this sense, the presence of structural and agential strategies to exclude, occlude, preclude, and ostracize sections of the public are giveaways that objectives other than open liberal democratic ones are being pursued in policy activities (Legrand & Jarvis, 2014).

The investigation of such illiberal activities, however, suffers from a weak analytical vocabulary and a lack of concepts that can aid analysis and discussion.

Here we propose the use of the terms set out earlier such as *policy risk, policy volatility*, and *policy malignancy* as a means to marshal the existing range of theoretical and conceptual viewpoints on the darkside and explore the reasons

Bad Public Policy 17

behind policy success and failure and their contribution to it. Use of these concepts to better understand hitherto omnipresent but neglected aspects of contemporary policy-making helps to create a shared research agenda for the policy sciences in examining both its own conduct and that of the sponsors of their investigations.

Specifically, we draw from recent work in policy studies that draws attention to these kinds of behaviors. On malign agents and their strategies in the policy process, for example, Allan McConnell's work identifies practices such as the development of "hidden agendas" in policy-making – policies with covert aims behind their ostensible purpose – and provides an insightful guide on how to proceed in their elaboration (McConnell, 2018). Plehwe and Günaydin (2022) provide another example, expanding on the idea of "destructive policy" where self-interested actors occupy niche policy positions that allow them to control or influence many aspects of policy analysis, its content, and application. They especially draw attention to how malevolent actors can sabotage a policy process or pursue the deliberate strategy of the "production of ignorance" in order to deceive policy-makers/takers, as they argued recently occurred, for example, in reforms to the German energy system (Plehwe & Günaydin, 2022).

Legrand (2022) has also developed a set of ideas and an analysis of malign policies in the area of national security that are exemplary. He examined how officials in Australia manipulated the terms and structures of debates in that country and elsewhere in order to diminish public scrutiny and exclude voices critical of security state initiatives. Opacity in policy settings can also help create uncertainty and insecurity. This is a subject Stefan Bachtold examined in his work on the control of social media in Myanmar in the effort to damp down discontent with regime activity, from the Rohingya genocide to opposition to a recent military coup (Bächtold, 2022).

Taylor, McDonnell, and Duong (2022), on the other hand, have focused attention on "bureaucratic gaming," drawing out civil servant's deliberate use of dubious practices in order to gain an advantage over one's competitors, gain personal prestige and budget maximization, among other non-Panglossian goals and ambitions.

Others like Weaver (2010) have taken the lead in considering how compliance and non-compliance affect policy expectations and how better understandings of target motivations and behavior are needed to inform more effective policy design efforts.

In addition to simply describing, diagnosing, and emphasizing these behaviors and outcomes, this emerging body of work also includes a budding literature that outlines possible correctives for these kinds of behavior. Several works, for example, have highlighted better methodological means for assessing the risks of policy failure (Jensen, 2022), while others have suggested possible correctives or solutions to the impasse of Panglossian policy advice in the face of a decidedly non-Panglossian world, such as, whenever possible, enhancing opportunities for public participation and crowd-sourcing (Howlett et al., 2022; Lee & Moon, 2022).

First Principles: The Public Interest and Public Policy

There is little doubt that almost all policy scholars have in common the aspiration to enhance or build an ever-improving apparatus and process for instituting political will for the public good (Douglas et al., 2021). Yet while a fervent hope of many is that public policy will reflect and institutionalize *the best expression of the public interest possible at the moment* – indeed much of the literature is oriented toward this aim – the evidence that it sometimes does not accomplish this aim or, in fact, does the opposite, is unfortunately abundant.

Any brief survey of politics in the world, for example, reveals a litany of public officials and members of the public engaged in malfeasant, corrupt, or malign behaviors. Governments of all stripes often abuse their position to institute preferential treatment of some citizens and marginalize others; while authoritarian figures pulling the levers of the state security establishment to suppress opposition is far from unknown. Scandals of many different types and impacts are common in the policy world.

These kinds of actions are often blatant but also often hidden or are covered with the veil of legitimacy assigning them a *prima facie* purpose that gives a government or government official the pretext of seeking public value. For example, in many countries after 9/11 new "security imperatives" have enabled "sustained measures to silence and even choke civil society" (UN, 2019), and the United Nations Human Rights Commission (UNHRC) has recognized that authoritarian states regularly apply "terrorist" labels to legitimize "excessive restrictions on the right to freedom of expression," "torture and ill-treatment," "to repress human rights defenders," and apply a "chilling effect on minorities, activists, [and] political opposition." Fundamental democratic norms, such as those stipulated by the International Covenant on Civil and Political Rights – the freedom of expression, the right of peaceful assembly, and the right to freedom of association – are commonly extinguished by both liberal and authoritarian regimes in this way (UN Rapporteur, 2019).

Such cynical acts are, of course, illiberal and anti-democratic and certainly not exercised in the public interest. But while these acts have not gone unnoticed, nor have they attracted as much scholarly attention in the policy sciences as they deserve. Rather this is a novel and somewhat aberrant theme for the discipline. This despite, as we have seen, that interest in the "darkside" or

Bad Public Policy

malignity in public policy can be traced to the very origins and establishment of "policy sciences" in the work of Harold Lasswell: the progenitor of many of our discipline's first principles who famously wrote on "who gets what, where and when" as the essence of politics and policy-making (Lasswell, 1936).

The present array of textbook approaches to studying policy-making, however, does not align well with the original Lasswellian vision, which recognized the need for determined action to overcome a wide variety of problems of this type. This is especially the case in the US – a country with enormous influence over the direction of many scholarly disciplines – where approaches to studying public policy have in past eras been dominated by the economics discipline, including in the contemporary era a significant influence from behavioral economics in particular (Friedman, 2002; Shafir, 2013), which contains a strong and overly rationalist predisposition.

The positivist inclination of economics and the application of causal explanatory models – often, but not always underpinned by an effort to develop and evaluate falsifiable hypotheses and/or the use of statistical calculus – has been the dominant if not default epistemology and methodology in US schools of public policy following their origin in the 1960s (Howlett & Jarvis, 2021). Although scholars' theoretical stances on knowledge and truth have always been a site of contestation, for more positivistic approaches in the policy sciences there has been one notable structural consequence of this epistemology: a stripping away from the analysis of the role of values and norms in policy-making in the pursuit of more elegant description of causality in social systems and policy outputs derived from empirical data analysis.

As mentioned earlier, however, a more recent generation of scholars has turned their attention beyond economics and the frailties embodied in economically inspired wards less positivistic methods and assumptions in order to help better understand why some policies succeed while others fail, raising the analysis of "bad" policies to the fore (Botterill & Fenna, 2019; Crowley et al., 2020; Leong & Howlett, 2022).

For these scholars, public policy is seen as a subject that can easily be turned to serve the less than benign interests that Lasswell warned of, or otherwise misappropriated in the pursuit of private gain and personal interest. Howlett et al. (2020), for example, are critical of policy scholars who take for granted the integrity of policy-makers and identify the "darkside" of policy processes as one in which adverse special interests, both among policy-makers and policy takers, are served. Likewise, Whiteford writes of "intentional harms" caused by policies aimed at punishing or otherwise singling out specific individuals and groups (Whiteford, 2021). For these scholars, and others like them, policy analysis is poorly served by Pollyannaish assumptions that policy-makers are entirely motivated by and serve the public interest in the pursuit of public value or, in the case of corrupt actors, adequately constrained in these proclivities by existing systems of checks-and-balances and other institutional arrangements established ostensibly to ensure transparency and accountability in government.

This next section brings together these two dimensions – the *public interest* and *liberal democratic institutions* – with a third, *legitimacy*, to create a general analytical framework for the understanding and analysis of malignity as a source of policy volatility. Its purpose in doing so is three-fold. First, to combine the common but often disparate enterprise among scholars of similar phenomenon. Second, to elucidate a conceptual *lingua franca* and compound these common contributions with notions of public value and bad policy. And, third, to sketch out the beginnings of an analytical approach capable of surfacing malign policy practices, exposing them to scrutiny, and showing how to mitigate them with robust instruments and policy designs that are built on coherent cognitive and normative grounds.

The foundation of this approach is normative in the Lasswellian sense insofar as it appeals to liberal democratic principles, the public interest, and public policy legitimacy. It seeks to advance effective policy-making that is aligned with the principles of good governance and expose behaviors that are not. By bringing together conceptual possibilities and normative values in a framework for analysis which informs the remainder of the Element, this section is intended to establish a theoretical beachhead for policy scientists working on, and against, the "darkside" of public policy.

Bad Policies and the Role of the Public

Across the world today, open and transparent government in the public interest is on the decline. Freedom House, for example, reported that 2022 was the seventeenth consecutive year of decline or "backsliding" in global democracy. Now more than 2.5 billion people live in illiberal or authoritarian countries, with severe limits on fundamental freedoms of association, speech, and assembly and many opportunities for the emergence of bad policy. China's persecution of its Uyghur population has been called a "cultural genocide"; Saudi Arabia has arbitrarily imprisoned dissenters and murdered its citizens overseas (such as the US-based journalist Jamal Khashoggi); in Egypt and Iran political opponents and LGBTQIA+ activists are blacklisted as terrorists; in Venezuela and Turkey opposition legislators are labelled enemies of the state and jailed; and in Russia human rights workers are expelled, and NGOs targeted by "foreign agents" laws.

In many of these states, such authoritarian oppression has stretched back decades. Yet, in many more there is a slide away from *liberal* democracy toward "*illiberal*" democracy and worse. These are states with elected governments, from Thailand to Hungary, which now only loosely adhere to the rule of law,

Bad Public Policy 21

react with violence to political dissent, and traduce civil rights (Bell & Jayasuriya, 1995; Zakaria, 2007). Freedom House (2018) has warned that such illiberalism is becoming "the new normal" across much of the globe and defined it as "an ideological stance that rejects the necessity of independent institutions as checks on the government and dismisses the idea of legitimate disagreement in the public sphere." In these states, politics and public policy scholars are increasingly tracking populist governments' systematic attempts to dismantle human (Roth, 2017), LGBTQIA+ (Krasteva, 2017), and citizenship rights among others (Howard, 2010) while introducing punitive measures against asylum seekers, journalists, political opponents, ethnic or religious minorities, and more.

This backsliding reminds us that it is important to be mindful of the different roles the "public" plays in "public policy" in both liberal democracies states and in non-democratic regimes.

That is, liberalism promotes the idea of civil society where the public can be found and of a demarcation of rights between the state and the individual which supports it. Bitonti notes that the very notion of the "public" bloomed with the creation of the modern Liberal state: "following the affirmation of the modern state, of the liberal idea of rule of law, and of individual rights, to be 'protected' and kept separated from the sphere of the public authority" (p. 3, 2019). It is for this reason that most ideas of "good" public policy hold the advancing of the public, rather than the state or purely individual, interests as its central conceit. In alternate state arrangements, from autocracy to authoritarianism and tyranny, a different idea of the "public interest" exists in which, typically, it is associated with the state, rather than civil society. In such regimes the "public" in the sense the term is used in liberal democracies is not necessarily central to the aim or outcome of public policy. Rather, it is the affairs and interests of the state that dominate, and these are neither necessarily commensurate nor coterminous with those of the "public" as democracies know it.

Few countries are immune from the real or potential malign wielding of state power; however, any identification of the public interest with the state can exacerbate these risks. A recent Special Issue of the journal *Policy Studies*, for example, was dedicated to identifying the impacts of Donald Trump's first presidency on US democracy within a framework which focused on efforts to create an "Imperial Presidency" and diminish civil society organizations and goals. Paula D. McLein, for example, traced the impact of Trump's racist rhetoric and policies, which "appeared to set out to exacerbate and inflame racial issues", pitting one group of citizens against another in a classic malign effort (2022). In the same issue, Foa and Monk argued that under Trump, the US shifted toward "dirty" democracy in which, as in many lesser developed countries or those led by military juntas or single-party states, decision-makers sought to transform the rules of democracy to suit their own benefit rather than that of the public.

Wider afield, many other scholars have also charted a global rise in populism closely associated with such actions as banning interest groups and NGOs that oppose the ideas and practices of the incumbent government, all the while professing to do so "in the larger public interest" (e.g. Albertazzi & McDonnell, 2015; Norris & Inglehart, 2019).

The scholarly work that charts these excesses and abuses of states is important and extensive. Yet, it has not penetrated very far into policy studies, and for those working in the policy field, there is a need to develop and mature unifying concepts that capture the often egregious excesses of states against their own citizens and incorporate those concepts into the orthodoxy of the policy sciences.

The Normative Orientation of Classical Policy Analysis and Its Contemporary Iteration

Notwithstanding Lasswell's injunction at the outset of the policy sciences discipline that it should remain "explicitly normative" and recognize its biases, the tendency for many in the discipline has been to focus instead on the diagnostic assessment of the factors and barriers that affect the realization of aims in policy and to develop advice on how to rectify those obstacles, *regardless of the goals and objectives at stake*. Among those taking a value-neutral position, for example, Dunn suggested that policy analysis is

> an applied social science discipline which uses multiple methods of inquiry and argument to produce and transform policy-relevant information that may be utilized in political settings to resolve policy problem (Dunn, 2013).

There is little doubt that the preponderance of research in the field is concerned with modelling and creating generalizable insights secured from an ostensibly scientific and dispassionate engagement with policy-making in order to make the policy process more efficient, more effective, and preferably both (in addition to the classic critique of Mead, 1985, see Farr, Hacker & Kazee, 2006; Durnová & Weible, 2020). Much of this work simply assumes that liberal democratic safeguards are in place and the policy context conducive to the attainment of public value in the public interest. But, of course, such a managerial approach will still apply even if the problem involves less the provision of better healthcare for all members of society than the efficient location and jailing of opposition members. That is, an emphasis on capacity, efficiency, and effectiveness often ignores both empirical and normative questions of "effectiveness for what," "to what end," and "for whom"?

Bad Public Policy   23

But this has not always been the case in the policy sciences, and warnings about the propensity to promote the development of a "value-free" policy science have been many. Peter deLeon, for example, noted in the early 1990s that reliance on neo-classic economic concepts afflicted the policy sciences with "an over reliance on instrumental rationality," which combined with "the complexity of the problem contexts" has led increasingly to a top-down and "increasingly technocratic, undemocratic orientation" (1994, p. 82).

The consequence of this stance toward policy analysis has been profound. John Dryzek, notably, has argued that "most policy analysis efforts to date are in fact consistent with an albeit subtle policy science of tyranny," by which he means "any elite-controlled policy process that overrules the desires and aspirations of ordinary people" (Dryzek, 1989, p. 98).

Studies primarily concerned with the questions of *how* the state exercises decision-making through institutions and administers those policy decisions often neglect the question concerning the reasons *why* they were enacted. For more critical policy scholars, however, policies (and those that create them) reveal much about the nature of power relations in society. A substantial element of many policy studies, for example, is concerned with the merits of different analytical approaches – the production of forensic understanding of how policies are created, applied, and their outcomes. But, as McConnell has noted, for positivist and empirical work: "where the focus is on the observable and measurable, it is anathema to conceive of variables whose existence is hidden from view" (p. 1741), including the normative nature of state-societal relations among others.

In fact, whether and how policy scholars engage with such normative questions currently divides the policy sciences (see Wagle, 2000). The recent emergence of "post-positivist," and critical or interpretivist scholarship as a counterpoint to the positivist orthodoxy, for example, was spurred by, and has promoted increased interest in engagement with the role of values and beliefs in policy-making rather than solely with concerns around issues related to evidence or efficiency (Perl et al., 2018).

Discursive, interpretivist, or constructivist scholars have all promoted a vision of policy-making that highlights the rich mix of beliefs, values, identities, and traditions that inform the lived experiences – and indeed the conflicts – of society. They argue that analysis of these elements of policy-making should be used to inform a deeper understanding of the social world than is typically provided by existing orthodox "positivist" policy science. In a recent issue of *Critical Policy Studies*, for example, editors Jennifer Dodge, Laureen Elbert, and Regina Paul argued we live in "times of turmoil" but call on critical policy scholars to "identify, situate, and critique contemporary crisis narratives." "Such analysis," they argue, "continues to be the foundation for articulating democratic alternatives for governing in ways that generate (globally) inclusive societal progress" (2022, p.132). Other scholars working in more positivist directions have similarly mounted sustained criticism of prevailing approaches to the field (Botterill & Fenna, 2019), arguing that current studies often fixate on minutiae while missing the big picture of government intent and its correspondence, or not, with the public interest.

This epistemological and methodological criticism of the policy sciences, even in liberal democratic states, has led to greater efforts in many countries to secure enhanced civil society participation in policy-making through activities such as "co-design," "co-creation," "co-management," and co-production. These concepts and processes all seek to better integrate state and civil society actors in the policy formulation, decision-making, and implementation processes. If such activities are needed in liberal democracies already structured and sworn to promote civil society, their need is that much greater in countries and regimes that actively discourage it.

This view of states, societies, and public policy animates the scholars and scholarship that informs the framework for understanding bad policy set out here.

Policy Success and Failure: Re-Stating the Public Policy and Policy Design Problematic in Intentional Terms

The nature of policy goals and their relationship to the means selected to achieve them lies at the heart of public policy-making and policy analysis. The importance of the normative dimension of these goals and aims is sometimes obscured when policies are described as technical or managerial decisions. Thus, Michael Howlett and M. Ramesh, for example, argue the policy literature often defines policy in this way whereby "[p]ublic policy is, at its most simple, a choice made by a government to undertake some course of action" (2003, p. 3). As they note, Thomas Dye's elegant and popular depiction that policy is "anything a government chooses to do or not do" (1972, p. 2) does not differentiate between beneficial and malicious goals. Others, however, are more insistent on the normative nature of policy-making. Hence, Frank Fischer, for example, makes a deeper claim about the link between values and facts in policy decision-making, stating that "public policies are essentially political agreements designed for the practical world of social action where facts and values are inextricably interwoven" (Fischer, 1980, p. 2). Goodin et al. go even further, specifying that "ruling is an assertion of the will, an attempt to exercise control, to shape the world. (and) Public policies are instruments of this assertive ambition [. . .]" (2006, p. 3).

Bad Public Policy 25

Centering public policy on ruling without a concern for ethics and norms has serious repercussions for policy analysis. First, democratic expression, (if it means anything), means the alignment of the public will with state-administered outcomes, incorporating a distinct vision of what it means to rule and how it should be done. To the extent that government decisions draw from the input of, or sanction from, the public – through democratic avenues – they are accorded *legitimacy*, something Fritz Scharpf describes as "a socially sanctioned obligation to comply with government policies even if these violate the actor's own interests or normative preferences, and even if official sanctions could be avoided at low cost" (Scharpf, 2003, p. 2).

Legitimacy is a concern central to the probity of a good policy process both in liberal democratic regimes and in other forms of government. Public access to, and participation in, political decision-making is often central to whether political outcomes are regarded by that public as having legitimacy. Indeed, in the converse the removal or suppression of public input diminishes that legitimacy (Scharpf, 1999). Similarly, the perception of unfairness, of some policy-makers and policy takers benefitting from "gaming" the system through the exclusion of others, is also antithetical to legitimacy (Hibbing and Theiss-Morse, 2002).

In democratic systems, in order to generate legitimacy, the public will is mediated by and through institutions, quantified by an electoral system, embodied in a political layer of elected representatives from which an executive is formed that in turn instructs an administrative apparatus to implement its program of activity, directing state and societal resources to the pursuit of some ends and not others.

This is a complex system and there is much to go wrong in public policy, of course. And simply enacting legitimate policies does not guarantee their success. The world is beset by hazards to the achievement of government's intentions, and whether through error or complexity, policy failure is a real and ever-present danger to governments of all stripes. Liberal democracy's 18th-century progenitors and 20th-century boosters include a procession of thinkers from Thomas Paine, John Locke, and Thomas Hobbes to Jean-Jacques Rousseau, John Stuart Mill, Jurgen Habermas, and John Rawls who grappled with this issue. These authors variously advocated for the advancement and preservation of individual freedoms and rights, a limit to the power of the state, equality of all before the law, an open society, universal suffrage, and more as pre-conditions for good policy.

Another subject towards which much scholarly work on policy-making is dedicated is towards overcoming or accommodating the uncertainty that arises in complex decision-making (see Sanderson, 2009). Some uncertainty about future states and continuing support for rulers, for example, never disappears. It remains an inherent problem and issue for any government, of any type and at any level, which must grapple with this uncertainty on a daily basis. It colors the attainment of goals in many ways both profound and mundane and is a subject that is discussed in much more depth in succeeding sections, including discussion of common techniques deployed by governments to deal with or mitigate its vicissitudes.

Other concerns go beyond a simple analysis of temporal uncertainty – the causes of which are usually beyond the gift of policy-makers to control. The latter often involve crises and risks that can be at least partially ascertained. In the former, however, a failure to serve the public interest often results less from unintended and unexpected external events and occurrences than from more easily foreseeable and preventable, but not well understood, internal ones (Howlett, 2012; Leong & Howlett, 2022).

In the latter case, it is typically the *deliberate* or intentional diversion of the state's administrative apparatus and resources that prevents an alignment between the public interest and public policy. This includes any policy that is employed to erode the foundational norms of liberal democracy.

Opening the Space for Malign Policy-Making: Difficulties in Assessing the Public Interest

If principles of good government values are the enduring destination of the vessel of the modern state, knowing the public interest is to chart a course through the day-to-day maelstroms and treacherous rocks of uncertainty and legitimacy toward that destination. But identifying the public interest when it is an aggregate of differing views can be a futile exercise, made more difficult by the fact that the public interest is neither homogenous nor static.

The public interest is generally seen as the spring or the source from which all good government action is mandated. *Salus populi suprema lex esto* – the health of the people should be the supreme law – is Cicero's famous maxim, yet determining or aggregating that interest meaningfully is not so straightforward. In *Public Opinion*, Walter Lippman reflects at length on "The making of the Common Will," asking: "How are those things known as the Will of the People, or the National Purpose, or Public Opinion to crystallize out of such fleeting and casual imagery?" (1946, p. 125). John Dewey, further, noted the difficulties associated with the concept, arguing that: "In no two ages or places is there the same public. Conditions make the consequences of associated action and the knowledge of them different" (1954,

p. 33), and Dewey asks, "What is the public? If there is a public, what are the obstacles in the way of its recognizing and articulating itself? Is the public a myth?" (1954, p.123).

Nevertheless, in the contemporary era Pal & Maxwell observe that

> the concept of a public interest is indispensable to a modern democracy, which presumes that public policy is to be undertaken in the interests of the entire community (or at least a substantial majority), not one section of that community (2004, p.3).

As Bitonti argues, however, realizing the notion of the "public interest" is difficult as the term has multiple connotations and is rhetorically deployed to:

(i) "define the essence of interest groups (analytical–theoretical function)";
(ii) "explain individual or collective actions (analytical–hermeneutic function)"; and,
(iii) "frame issues persuasively (practical–conative function)" (Bitonti, 2020).

Wheeler's reflection on this question resorts to a process-and-objective definition that is critical:

> The public interest is best seen as the objective of, or the approach to be adopted, in decision-making rather than a specific and immutable outcome to be achieved. The meaning of the term, or the approach indicated by the use of the term, is to direct consideration and action away from private, personal, parochial or partisan interests towards matters of broader (i.e., more "public") concern (Wheeler, 2006, p. 24).

This causes many difficulties in policy analysis and policy-making, opening up room for the equation of the concept with private or party interest or for its misspecification and obfuscation. This "space" between the actual public interest and what it is claimed to be is the space in which malign actors operate and bad policies emerge.

The Less-than-Altruistic Policy Taker

Most of the limited existing literature examining bad policies has focused on policy-makers, including their sometimes corrupt and self-interested or heavily partisan propensities. But there is also another large area of concern: that related to adverse or malicious behavior of policy "takers" evading or otherwise undermining government initiatives. This behavior on the part of policy takers to deceive, "game," or otherwise evade the intentions and expectations of government when "complying" with regulations, subsidies, and other forms of government action is a subject often entirely glossed over in studies of policy-making.

In most orthodox policy studies consideration of such "target behaviour" is commonly couched in utilitarian language and assumptions (Howlett, 2018), and the idea commonly found in the policy literature is that the only real issue involved with policy-takers is whether or not they comply willingly with government orders and advice. This subject is then thought to consist mainly of "getting incentives (and disincentives) right," with expected target behavior anticipated to be sure to follow when this occurs (Howlett, 2018).

This not only ignores both aspects of the social and political construction of policy targets as, for example, "worthy" or "deviant," but also affects how they are treated (Schneider & Ingram, 1990a, 1990b) and minimizes the complex behaviors that go into compliance on the part of any citizen. These involve most notably considerations of the legitimacy of state or public action, but also those related to cupidity, trust, and the operation of a wide variety of descriptive and injunctive social norms that affect policy taker behavior (Bamberg & Moser, 2007; Thomas et al., 2016; Howlett, 2019; Weaver, 2014, 2015).

It is very common in the policy sciences, for example, to view policy takers as static targets who do not try, or at least do not try very hard, to evade policies or even to profit from them in unexpected or unanticipated ways (Braithwaite, 2003; Marion & Muehlegger, 2007; Howlett, 2019). But such behaviors on the part of policy takers are often key in determining the success or failure of many government initiatives from tobacco control and drug addiction to bus fare evasion and food stamp fraud (Delbosc & Currie, 2016; Kulick et al., 2016).

Compliance is often thought of as purely an "implementation" issue and left up to administrators to deal with rather than forming an essential component of policy formulation and design (Doig & Johnson, 2001; Kuhn & Siciliani, 2013). Many policy designs, for example, have been developed with only the most rudimentary and cursory knowledge of how compliance relationships operate or how specific kinds of policy tools and behaviors are likely to interact and change over time (Kiss et al., 2013; Taylor et al., 2013). However, these should be "designed for" in the sense that determined non-compliance and other similar behaviors – from free-ridership to fraud and misrepresentation (Harring, 2016) – must be taken into account in formulating policies and constructing policy designs designed to counteract or minimize their occurrence. There is a need to "design in" correctives such as stricter accountability mechanisms, verification, and monitoring plans right at the outset in order to ensure these are locked in and left in place as the program or policy matures (Vine & Sathaye, 1999; Plaček & Ochrana, 2018).

Some work on this subject does exist, however, and can serve as a starting point for the analysis of how to deal with volatile designs. When policy tools are utilized which are subject to gaming, fraud, or misrepresentation on the part of policy-takers, for example, it is clear that additional resources are required to build in the accountability, monitoring, and auditing functions required for such mixes to operate effectively (Blanc, 2018). Designs based on nodality and nudges and/or treasure resources such as those often most closely associated with modern collaborative governance, for example, are always highly volatile as the opportunities in such arrangements are ripe for cheating and gaming and protections against such behavior often rely only on trust.

There is thus a need to better assess and address the risks of failure right at the outset when a policy is first considered (Falco, 2017; Taylor et al., 2019). It is necessary to have better and continuous monitoring and assessment or evaluation of policy impacts and outcomes, and the ability to respond to any compliance deficits with new tools or altered calibrations of existing ones as well as a clear sense of what it is that motivates those impacted by policies if desired levels of compliance are to be realized.

A Brief Analytical Framework for the Study of Bad Policy

The position outlined above aligns with Weaver's (2014 and 2015) admonition that designers need to think not in terms of compliance, per se, but rather in terms of "compliance regimes" in which different policy targets can be treated in different ways depending on the actual behavior envisioned and encountered. Doing so, however, requires a high level of policy knowledge, skill, and capacity on the part of government, and capacity building in this area may be required as a pre-requisite (Howlett, 2015; Wu et al., 2015).

Furthering the study of the darkside of policy-making and the mitigation of propensities to develop bad policy requires an analytical framework helping to set out the origins of the problem and suggesting these and additional routes toward the mitigation of problems in the area. Such analytical frameworks are valuable in identifying social phenomenon, discerning these against the background "noise" and cohering the underlying claim so that it might be validated, negated, challenged, transformed, or enhanced by subsequent scholarly investigation.

For a framework to be useful, it must:

- define the phenomenon at hand and distinguish it from similar or related phenomenon,
- define the concepts and the relationships between them that describe the phenomenon, and
- provide some form of categorization for relevant data informing the concepts (Pal & Maxwell, 2004).

In their work Pal and Maxwell provide a framework of approaches to the question of the public interest, which is quite useful for helping to clarify the role of the public interest in policy-making, both good and bad (see Table 1). Here they distinguish between processes that further the public interest, the role of majority opinion as a mechanism for determining its content, the role of utilitarian calculations in promoting it, and the idea that the public interest must be in some sense "common" and based on shared values.

This framework is useful since it shows how each of these factors and elements can be distorted away from the public and toward other interests, namely state or organizational or individual ones, resulting in poor or "bad" policies (Vargas Cullell, 2004, p. 97). The analysis of bad policy outlined in Table 2 is premised on its disregard or distortion of these qualities.

Policies that by design, intent, or outcome erode or skirt around the principles of good government in the public interest are malign. This includes policies that interfere with, diminish, or denigrate the rule of law or personalize power in society and rule in the rulers' self-interest.

Such policies can be promoted by various factions in society and can emerge at any time. Their existence demonstrates the capacity, and willingness, of even advanced liberal democracies to sidestep their core values and exist as a perennial threat to the continual operation of liberal democratic systems, and

Table 1 Approaches to the public interest (Pal & Maxwell, 2004)

Process	Focus on procedures as the basis for arriving at decisions in the public interest – fair representation of all interests; transparency; legality; due process; etc.
Majority Opinion	The guide to regulatory decisions is what a significant majority of people think about an issue.
Utilitarian	Tries to balance different interests in the process to arrive at a solution that maximizes benefits for society as a whole but also is a compromise of different direct interests represented in that process representations to the regulatory agency.
Common Interest	The guide here is a pragmatic interest that the public has in common – for example, public goods such as clean air, water, defense, public safety, an innovative economy
Shared Value	Shared values as the basis for interests, but also an ethical guide for decision-makers

Table 2 Characteristics of policy alignment and misalignment

Aspect of the Public Interest Involved	Observed	Ignored
Institutions (values embedded therein)	Free and fair elections, recognition and protection of human rights, the rule of law, a free press, the separation of powers, and the protection of minority interest	Rigged or gerrymandered elections, erosion of human rights, traducing rule of law, suppressing freedom of press
Process (public interest articulated through)	Participatory, majority opinion, utilitarian, common interest, shared value	Exclusionary, unilateral, opaque, or lip-service to process
Outcomes (legitimacy accrues within)	Transparency of process, non-exclusionary input mechanisms; results in high public trust	Exclusionary, secretive, obstructive, results in low public trust

the notions of good government in the public interest that go with it. Thus in the wake of the UK's referendum that cemented the country's exit from the EU, for example, when the British high court ruled that it was Parliament, and not the Prime Minister, that was ultimately capable of triggering Article 50 to commence the process the tabloid newspaper the Daily Mail published a front-page article with photographs of the three judges above the headline that should alarm any supporter of an independent judiciary: "Enemies of the People." Not long after that, the UK government confirmed that it intended to "break international law in a very specific and limited way" to implement its legislation for the UK's internal market. In 2022, a report by the All Party Parliamentary Group on Democracy and the Constitution confirmed that "since at least 2016, the government has increasingly attacked judges," is "constitutionally unhelpful and inappropriate," and "may also have created the impression that the Supreme Court has been influenced by ministerial pressure."

This kind of breach is antithetical to good government and good policy-making but is unfortunately quite common. Verisk Maplecroft's *Judicial Independence Index* in 2021, for example, identified interference in the judiciary in forty-five countries, including EU member states Poland and the Czech

Republic, and Switzerland – where the top court Swiss judges are elected by their political party, an arrangement described as "fragile."

A second major concern exists with exclusion from decision-making, which also occurs all too frequently, notwithstanding many protestations to the contrary (LeGrand 2022).

Such exclusion of sections of the public can be understood in four dimensions. First as *occlusion*, which refers to the intentional concealment of information relevant to the public's assessment of the performance of political elites who are accountable to the public. Second, as *preclusion*, which describes deliberate attempts to restrict or deny a citizen's means of participating in democratic exercises, such as by hindering their input, standing, or access to those exercises. Third, *ostracism* involves framing an individual or group as disloyal to the interests of the community at large, either through direct or indirect encouragement by the community itself, and finally, exclusion can appear as *excision*, which represents the most extreme form of removing citizen access to or participation in a democracy, such as through the suspension or revocation of democratic processes, institutions, or rights.

Such modes of exclusion and perceptions of unfairness are, Legrand argues, inherently malign in any regime and commonly lead to or are combined with a lack of transparency that also contributes to poor policies and poor outcomes.

None of these problems should be ignored. Rather attending to these forms of malignity wards malign directs our attention to modes of decision-making that "can involve policy instruments that deny or delay access to the political arena, or voice within that arena, to ideas or agents of a certain economic, ethnic, social, political or religious provenance" (Legrand, 2022, p. 96).

Conclusion: Building Knowledge about Bad Policy

Many liberal democracies have regressed in the past twenty years as part of a "democratic recession" linked in part to growing political polarization and an inability to locate and rule in the public interest (Carothers & O'Donohue, 2019). Polarization, it is often argued, contributes to rising intolerance, discrimination, and violence, while reducing trust, undermining participation, and creating space for malign and malicious policies. As Carothers and O'Donohue warn, the risk of polarization to societies is that it "weakens respect for democratic norms, corrodes basic legislative processes, undermines the nonpartisan stature of the judiciary, and fuels public disaffection with political parties."

But trust and legitimacy are always and at all times crucial to liberal democracies – together they form what Rosanvallon (2008) describes as an "invisible institution," or "a property of a relationship between persons or groups, for example, between governors and governed" (p. 48), which contributes heavily to good policy-making. In liberal democracies, in particular, it is vital that trust is "built and maintained, guaranteed in short, if it is to endure" (p. 48).

This section has set out an analytical framework and set of concepts that understands how the value of individual autonomy, freedom and rights, the rule of law and a limited state can be preserved and enhanced or undermined and rolled-back. These insights were tied to a discussion of "good" policy-making and policies and "bad" ones and how the two can be distinguished. This work helps to analytically uncover malign or malicious uses of the policy process as those directed towards other purposes than the promotion of the public interest, be they in the state-centric goals of authoritarian states or the individual self-interest of rulers in any type of regime.

4 The Inherent Vices of Policy and Policy Design

It is imperative for scholarly work in the policy sciences to study bad policy in a systematic and analytical fashion. The reasons for this are two-fold: first, it is crucial that the field avoid being complicit in the oppressive structures that blight many countries. Second, it is needed so as to actively build knowledge of the policy instruments and processes that can identify and mitigate harms and incorporate that knowledge into policy designs that can help guard against the risks faced by public policies.

Of course, the idea of malevolent actors utilizing the policy process and the powers of government for their own interests while neglecting the public interest is an old one and has been a major concern of political theorists, revolutionaries and reformists, and practicing politicians and critics for centuries. And the previous sections have already argued for this concern to be taken more seriously by contemporary policy scientists and students of public policy-making. However, this normative concern is not the only sense in which policies are "bad," and this section deals with a second major sense of the source of poor or unsuccessful policy – of inherent vices and policy design practices that do not mitigate their risks effectively. These vices or problems exist at all stages of the policy process and constitute a major series of challenges for policy makers and policy designs.

Policy analysts need better tools to better grapple with, and avoid, these additional sources of policy volatility, and this, in part, is what this Element is all about (Hoppe, 2018; Feldman, 2018; Viscusi & Gayer, 2015; Dudley & Xie,

2020). This section in particular builds on research in the areas of risk and risk management to show how these types of risks can be better identified and managed, if not entirely eliminated, and by so doing allow policy-making to be more effective (Dudley, 2022).

This section develops the study of these sources of bad policy by expanding upon the concepts of policy vices and policy volatility set out earlier and discusses their relevance for studies of, and thinking about, the policy design key component of policy-making (Howlett, 2024). It outlines several of the most prominent, and predictable, ways in which even laudable policy aims can be thwarted and bad policy emerges from the efforts of even the most well-intentioned governments. The section sets out these problems in more detail and stresses the need for improved risk management and mitigation strategies if their effects are to be reduced. This latter subject is then taken up again in Sections 5 and 6, including by examining the practices of several prominent national governments in attempting to do so.

Introduction: Policy Design and the Inherent Propensity of Policies to Fail

Policy design is a term used here to describe both a process of policy-making and an outcome of that process and can be defined as an arrangement of policy tools and resources (Hood, 1986) and "a specific form of policy formulation based on the gathering of knowledge about the effects of policy tool use on policy targets and the application of that knowledge to the development and implementation of policies" (Howlett, 2024).

Although design activity occurs mainly at the policy formulation stage of the policy process, it is not synonymous with that stage. Rather, it represents the process through which sets of ideas about policy-making and possible policy outcomes are combined and embodied in policy outcomes (Goggin, 1987; Howlett, 2024). As such, it is a key activity affecting how values and actor interests are incorporated into policy and is a common source or location of policy problems and failures (Leong and Howlett, 2022).

Although often studied, relatively little attention has been paid in the policy design literature to some of the inherent difficulties of policy-making cited above including, in addition to the presence of malevolent or self-interested actors discussed in previous sections, difficulties anticipating and preparing for uncertain future events and occurrences, unwelcoming political environments, policy-takers who fail to comply with government directives and policy-makers who fail to learn from past experiences. These contextual limitations and theoretical blindspots concern what we have referred to earlier as the "inherent vices" of policy-making. They are all factors that contribute to bad policy in the sense of policy likely to fail, increasing levels of policy volatility and elevating risks of policy failure.

This is surprising since the study of policy design is inextricably linked with the idea of creating policies through the conscious and systematic consideration of the likely outcomes of policy implementation activities. And bad polices are a concern both for non-governmental actors who bear the costs of government failures and incompetence and for governmental ones who may be tasked with carrying out impossible duties or meeting unrealistic expectations.

The activity of creating or designing a policy overlaps and straddles policy formulation, decision-making, and policy implementation and involves actors, ideas, and interests active at each of these stages of the policy process (Howlett et al., 2019). However, it also relies on a very specific form of interaction among these elements, one that is typically expected to be driven by knowledge and evidence of alternatives' merits and demerits in achieving policy goals rather than by other less evidence-intensive processes such as bargaining, personalistic agendas or electioneering among key policy actors (Bobrow & Dryzek, 1987; Bobrow, 2006; Howlett, 2024).

Like the panglossian vision of policy-making set out earlier, this vision of policy design processes assumes a well-intentioned government and typically ignores the darkside of policy-making, or even its strong normative nature, in favor of a more technocratic approach to the subject. Such a mode of designing policies, of course, is only one possible orientation or set of practices that can be followed in policy formulation and result in policy outputs (Tribe, 1972; Colebatch, 1998). Other less knowledge-based ones are sometimes referred to as "non-design" processes and are often more closely linked to political bargaining and negotiation (Howlett & Mukherjee, 2017). In the design case, policy formulators are typically expected as much as possible to base their analyses on logic, knowledge, and experience rather than, for example, purely political calculations and other forms of satisficing behavior, which also can serve to generate policy alternatives more susceptible to self-interested manipulation (Sidney, 2007; Bendor et al., 2009).

This technocratic view permeates the policy design literature. In their many works on the subject in the late 1980s and early 1990s, for example, Stephen H. Linder and B. Guy Peters argued that policy designs could be considered in the abstract as divorced from the actual process followed in public policy decision-making and studied as a subject in their own right. That is, that policies can be viewed in the same way that are many other human constructs, as the concrete manifestation of sets of ideas about utility and the creation of "affordances" enabling the better achievement of the goals of their creator.

Conceptually, however, a policy design process does begin with knowledge of the abilities of different kinds of policy tools to affect policy outputs and outcomes and of the kinds of resources required to allow those tools to operate as intended (Hood, 1986; Salamon, 2002). Designs contain both a substantive component – a set of alternative arrangements thought potentially capable of resolving or addressing some aspect of a policy problem, one or more of which is ultimately put into practice – and a procedural component – a set of activities related to securing some level of agreement among those charged with formulating, deciding upon, and administering that alternative vis-à-vis other alternatives (Howlett, 2024). And some knowledge of both of these elements is required in all cases, even if it is shallow and cursory.

This knowledge involves at minimum some understanding of the source of policy tool effects and how the use of different kinds of instruments affects target group behavior and compliance with government aims in specific ways in specific circumstances. And it also should include knowledge and consideration of the constraints on tool effectiveness originating in the limits of existing knowledge, prevailing constitutional, legal and governance structures, and other arrangements and behaviors which may preclude consideration of certain options and promote others whether appropriate to the context or not. Policy design in this sense is a process that requires propitious circumstances including relatively high levels of analytical skills and evidentiary capacity, as well as the intention to exercise those skills and capacity in the development and realization of a design.

The designs that emerge from such processes are often thought of as "ideal types," that is, as ideal configurations or sets of policy elements which can be developed independently of problems and which can reasonably be expected, within a specific contextual setting, to deliver a specific outcome, much like a design for a building or a ship. Whether or not all the aspects of a design are realizable in a specific contextual configuration in practice, in this view, is more or less incidental to the design, in the same way that a building budget or poor soil quality may not allow as grandiose a plan for a bank or headquarters or public building to be realized as was originally proposed by its architect or builder (Linder & Peters, 1988). Such building designs, however, should still deal with major risks such as those for fires, earthquakes, floods, or landslides, which are endemic to all buildings. Effective or 'good' policy designs, both in theory and in practice, should also deal with forseeable contingencies and risks that are well known and omnipresent.

As Linder and Peters (1990) argued, a more evidence-based design orientation to analysis can illuminate the variety of means implicit in policy alternatives, questioning the choice of instruments and their aptness in particular contexts. The central role it assigns means in policy performance may also be a normative vantage point for appraising design implications of other analytical approaches. More important, such an orientation can be a counterweight to the design biases implicit in other approaches and potentially redefine the fashioning of policy proposals.

This detailed and careful consideration of policy is the bread-and-butter of the design work undertaken by actors such as think tanks, policy institutes, policy schools, and the policy shops of government (Migone et al., 2024), and is the form practiced and advocated by many academics (Migone et al., 2022). But in many cases, however, the provision of design elements expected to mitigate or reduce policy risks, and volatility is not considered nor incorporated into design proposals and templates.

This is difficult to understand when policy actors such as think tanks or research institutes develop and propose alternatives to existing policy arrangements, often quite far in advance of when an issue will actually appear on a government agenda, and thus are able to propose more "rational" or evidence-based alternatives than when a problem suddenly arises. But when they attempt to develop new or revised solutions to potential or existing problems, solutions which are argued to be more likely to better achieve government or societal goals and/or to do so more effectively than present practices, they need also to consider the risks and potential problems associated with their proposals.

That is, designs differ not only in the types of means chosen and the nature of the goals they pursue but also in the quality of the logical or empirical relations postulated to exist between policy components, including their risks of failure. And this is not difficult to do since policies typically encounter several readily identifiable problems that can easily be modelled and anticipated. Proposed possible solutions to problems may be incorrect or ignored, the means expected to deal with a problem may be mis-specified or poorly executed if adopted, and problems and solutions may be poorly defined or mismatched.

Such errors are unavoidable if only poor knowledge of them exists or if they are ignored in the processes in place to match solutions with problems and vice versa. But they are also present even in the best of circumstances and always need to be addressed (Cohen et al., 1979; Eijlander, 2005; Franchino & Hoyland, 2009; Sager & Rielle, 2013). They are "inherent risks" that policy scholars and practitioners must take more seriously if bad policies are not to result from policy design processes.

Re-Thinking Policy Risks

There are many problems in policy-making that affect policy outcomes and serve as potential sources of failure or harbingers of success (McConnell, 2010). Many of these tendencies (some already well-observed and researched in fields such as micro- and behavioral economics (Friedman, 2002; Thaler, 2018; Chapman et al., 2021), if recognized, can be mitigated. But the current state of the art of policy and policy design studies does not engage in their analysis in a profound enough way to inform possible mitigation measures and ensure these are included in adopted designs.

As already noted, policy studies and studies of policy design to date have focused almost exclusively on activities that take place under "brightside" assumptions of the "right" conditions being present to allow for ideal policy discussions and considerations. But these conditions of well-intentioned and well-informed governments and accommodating policy targets are often lacking (Howlett, 2020a; Howlett, 2020b; Jarvis & Legrand, 2018). Not only are government decisions often undertaken in conditions of high uncertainty (Manski, 2011), but designs must deal with adverse behavior on the part of both policy-makers and policy-takers, which heighten uncertainty (Cox, 2019; Howlett, 2021, 2020).

Policy design thinking needs to address these kinds of risks head-on. They are not the typical "external" risks such as climate change or technological innovations that can upset existing policy regimes, but rather "internal" risks inherent to policy-making itself. The possibilities not just of uncertainty – a perennial problem highlighted in the literature on wicked problems, for example (Levin et al., 2012) – but also that policy-makers and policy takers, as discussed in earlier sections, are sometimes, or often, driven by malicious or venal motivations rather than socially beneficial or disinterested ones, are very problematic to a classical design orientation. The fact that policy targets have proclivities toward free-ridership, and rent-seeking rather than simply complying with government intentions (Taylor, 2021; Howlett, 2020) is also an omnipresent risk that can work to undermine policy effectiveness and which needs to be taken seriously in both policy-making in general and policy design efforts. These tendencies must be curbed for even well-intentioned policies to achieve their aims.

The Inherent Vices of Policy Design – Unpreparedness, Uncertainty, Maliciousness, Non-Compliance, and Non-Learning

In the sense in which the term is used in the insurance industry, an "inherent vice" refers to the quality of any substance or object that causes it to self-destruct, whether quickly or slowly (Rodda, 1949). Such vices are defined in relation to the risk a particular product or process faces such as the risk of fruit rotting in transit to markets (Leong & Howlett, 2022).

As was suggested in earlier sections, many flaws in policy designs can be thought to originate as the "inherent vices" of policies themselves (Leong & Howlett, 2022). Just as with art pieces, for example, policies also deteriorate as a function of incremental changes over time, such as when the policy tools or instruments that are combined in a policy design when a policy is created fail to deliver due to a change in their external environment. Or they may also be doomed from the start if no efforts at all are made to ensure they accommodate best evidence and practices or ensure they can adjust and adapt to changing conditions such as when a subsidy or welfare payment does not contain an automatic inflation adjustment and loses purchasing power over time. (Howlett, 2019). And just as in the case of ship or building design, understanding these inherent sources of failure is important to policy-making both in designing a policy and in the inclusion within it of measures to correct, offset or mitigate the risks of failure they entail (Howlett, 2012).

The extent to which these inherent problems and risks of policy-making feature in a policy design can be said to constitute its degree of *"volatility"* (Howlett & del Rio, 2016; Rogge & Reichardt, 2016). Just as in the financial sector, designs featuring volatile tool portfolios require additional efforts to be made to hedge or offset risk-meaning the inclusion of more and different kinds of policy instruments in order to reduce the risk profile of the primary set (Bali et al., 2021). When a policy requires the use of tools or contains elements that are often subject to gaming, or fraud, for example, additional tools are required to build in accountability, monitoring, and auditing functions if such policies are to operate effectively (Blanc, 2018).

The five key risks listed in Table 3 are *inherent* to policy-making in the sense that they are inevitable and built into the very fabric of public policy-making. They include "unpreparedness," "uncertainty," "maliciousness," "non-compliance," and "non-learning (Howlett, 2000; Lang, 2019) and affect the different kinds of tasks and activities involved in policy-making, including policy design.

Table 3 Risks inherent to each stage of policy-making

Stage of Policy Process	Principle Activity	Inherent Risk of Failure
Agenda-Setting	Issue Management	Unpreparedness, Surprise
Policy Formulation	Effective Design	Uncertainty
Decision-Making	Public Interest & Value	Malignity
Policy Implementation	Efficient Implementation	Non-Compliance
Policy Evaluation	Lesson-Drawing	Non-Learning

These are all important sources of policy failure and have received different degrees of treatment in the existing policy literature. "Unpreparedness", for example, has been the subject of much work on foresight and issue management in government (Leigh, 2003; van der Steen & Twist, 2013) while learning and "non-learning" has long been a problem in the bailiwick, and sights, of policy evaluation researchers (Wholey, Hatry, & Newcomer, 2010) and will not be discussed in depth here.

Rather, attention is focused on the three most neglected aspects of policy-making risk: uncertainties around policy problems, malicious decision-making, and the effects of poor public compliance with government intentions (Howlett & Mukherjee, 2019, 2017a).

The status of these three problems as "inherent vices" in policy-making is clear. With respect to uncertainty, as set out above, policies can deteriorate as a function of incremental changes over time in reaction to new stresses and strains. Decision-makers who know they operate within this context can try to reduce uncertainties to a manageable level, quite easily in some circumstances – such as when they are dealing with well-known or "tame" kinds of problems whose causes and solutions are well known (Parkhurst, 2016) – but not as well in others – such as novel viruses and pandemics, which upset existing routines and highlight unknown problems and solutions (Capano et al., 2020).

Second, not only are policy solutions and trajectories subject to uncertainties, but they are also subject to abuses and manipulations that can undermine their ability to resolve problems (Howlett, 2019). False, biased, incorrect, or misleading information can enter into political discussions over time and affect policy deliberations in undesirable ways (Simon, 1967, 1978; Dudley & Xie, 2020, 2022; Howlett, 2019; Jones, 2002). And the non-public interested behavior of policy makers examined in earlier sections can lead them to proliferate disinformation or place private or state gains ahead of the public good, again interfering with effective policy-making. Evidence of such malicious and malign policy behavior is embodied in the many forms of corruption, collusion, and clientelism that can affect policy-making (Dahlström et al., 2012; Legrand & Jarvis, 2014).

And thirdly, it is not just policy-makers but also policy takers or "targets" who may not conform with stereotypes or ideal wishes about the nature of expected policy compliance (Schneider & Ingram, 2005). "Targets" may comply with government intentions but can also evade, alter, or "vote with their feet" in many ways that fail to conform with government wishes (Weaver, 2010, 2014, 2015). This non-compliance can have significant consequences not only in areas such as drug addiction or smoking, which feature stubborn adherence to old habits regardless of the penalties and costs imposed by health authorities, but also in much more mundane circumstances such as tax evasion, or regulatory venue-shopping (Braithwaite, 2003; Yackee & Yackee, 2010).

Bad Public Policy

Each of the three neglected vices – uncertainty, maliciousness, and non-compliance – and the lessons from the existing literature concerning them, along with the implications of those findings for good and bad policy design, is discussed in more detail below.

Uncertainty

Uncertainty is an inherent vice of policy-making that has been widely studied in diverse disciplines from psychology to organization theory but only rarely in a policy context that tends to operate, as Manski (2011 and 2013) put it, "with incredible certitude." In the policy world, much of the limited discussion of uncertainty that exists has centered on the nature of what Simon (1973) termed "ill-structured problems" or issues in which the nature of policy problems and solutions are un- or little-known. The contrast between "wicked" and "tame" problems mentioned above, for example, has dominated thinking around the subject in the policy sciences and has influenced both policy studies and policy-making (Churchman, 1967; Head, 2008a; Levin et al., 2012; Rittel & Webber, 1973).

Such problem and solution-related unknowns, however, are only a part of a larger group of uncertainties policy-makers face (Morgan & Henrion, 1990; Howlett & Nair, 2017). Uncertainties surrounding the choice of policy options, their consequences, confidence in the quality of available information, and contested and poorly known or understood values of multiple stakeholders, including decision-makers, leave a great deal of ambiguity concerning what might be the correct action to follow in many cases, among other things allowing plentiful opportunities for self-interested interventions (Knight, 1921; Hansson, 1996; van der Sluijs, 2005).

Koppenjan and Klijn (2004) present a useful classification of such policy uncertainty focused on the interaction among actors and knowledge (or information)-related uncertainty for solving complex policy problems. They argue that three main types of uncertainty exist which policies and policy designs must address. These uncertainties relate not just to the presence or absence of policy frames and solutions but also to the issues and risks related to the "value-ladenness" of policy choices, which includes different actor perspectives on the *worth* and value of the knowledge and information being utilized for decision-making, and the quality and nature of the presentation of arguments concerning preferred policy alternatives and pathways (Webster, 2003; Head, 2008b; Mathijssen et al., 2008; Maxim & van der Sluijs, 2011).

These are:

1) *Substantive uncertainty* that relates to a lack of relevant information related to the nature of the complex problem, and the different

interpretations of information arising from different "frames of reference" of the social actors;
2) *Strategic uncertainty* that arises due to unpredictability of strategies deployed by different actors based on their perception of the problem and strategies likely to be deployed by other actors; and
3) *Institutional uncertainty* that arises owing to the complexity of interaction of different actors guided by institutional frameworks, that is, rules and procedures of the organizations they represent.

Strategies for better policy-making, therefore, need to understand these risks and policy designs need to encompass them. This involves more than just the need to be able to design and adopt policies that are agile and flexible enough to deal with relatively normal "wickedness" or uncertainty (Capano & Woo, 2018). In more turbulent circumstances, such as where policy ideas and actors change frequently, and opportunities for abuse proliferate, policies must also be designed to withstand active and determined efforts to undermine or distort them (Bauer & Knill, 2014; Jordan & Matt, 2014). This means policy designs and policy-making require additional and redundant resources and capabilities that allow them to change course as conditions change, including feedback mechanisms and procedures for automatic or semi-automatic adjustment in the face of changing circumstances and support (Baumgartner & Jones, 2002; Jacobs & Weaver, 2015; Pierson, 1992; Pierson, 1993).

Maliciousness

Policy studies have even more rarely dealt with the second inherent vice, that related to the desire of some self-interested parties, from decision-makers to policy targets, to hijack, distort, or otherwise re-orient public processes toward their own ends and goals often at the expense of others (Habermas, 1974; Jones, 2002; Perl et al., 2018).

The existence of this kind of behavior, and the malign policies which result from it, was discussed at length in earlier sections. Examples range from the use of public authority to promote the interests of ethnic, religious, and other favored groups or specific sets of "clients" (Gans-Morse et al., 2014; Goetz, 2007) or to penalize or punish others (Howlett et al., 2017). And they extend to the misuse of policies to enrich or otherwise benefit policy-makers and administrators themselves (Uribe, 2014), including manipulating target groups through vote-buying or other forms of electoral pandering (Brancati, 2014; Manor, 2013).

Most such perversions of the public interest can be corrected or mitigated through institutional and process reforms. Corruption, for example, is often found in organizations and can be managed through a combination of traditional monitoring and policing activity promoting accountability and transparency. The creation of anti-corruption agencies and the development of more effective financial and recruitment controls, for instance, are only two examples of such devices (Quah, 2007). These can also include regulations placing limits on party funding and careful monitoring and disclosure of government contracting and procurement activity to name only two others. However other forms of malicious or malign behaviour such as clientelism or ethnic favoritism require more robust institutions and processes and are much more difficult to defuse or mitigate.

(Non)Compliance

Thirdly, although many implementation studies have focused on problems related to administrative behaviors which lead to policy failures such as lengthy principle-agent chains (Ellig & Lavoie, 1995) and a range of "barriers to implementation" such as poor training and recruitment practices, very little of this work has penetrated into policy studies. These problems, from a lack of personnel or financial resources to burdensome historical practices and legal requirements, slow down or render implementation ineffective and have received some treatment in the field (Wu et al., 2017).

But these studies often fail to address other significant issues relating to the non-compliance of target populations with government intentions which is critical to effective policy design (Nilsen, 2015; Weaver, 2015; de Montis et al., 2016; Dowling & Legrand, 2023). While such behavior has been an essential component of studies in fields such as law and accounting (Doig & Johnson, 2001; Kuhn & Siciliani, 2013; Howlett, 2018) it has been glossed over in studies of public policy (Howlett, 2020, 2021).

Weaver (2009) termed this compliance problem "the final frontier" of implementation research. Adverse or malicious behavior of policy "takers" who fail to comply or pervert government wishes and frustrate their intentions are a serious, ever-present, and common problem (Taylor, 2021). Indeed, overcoming compliance problems is fundamental to implementation success (Profeti and Toth, 2025).

The accounts of the actions of bureaucrats and other implementers commonly found in the policy literature, however, often suggest that the only real issue in policy compliance is one of correctly calibrating incentives and disincentives to encourage policy targets to comply with government aims when other efforts at suasion have failed (Howlett, 2018). However, as set out earlier, this not only ignores many social and behavioral aspects involved in the social and political construction of targets (Schneider & Ingram 1990a; 1990b) but also minimizes the complex behaviors that go into compliance – from levels of trust, to other social and individual behavioral determinants such as acceptance and adherence to social norms (Bamberg & Moser, 2007; Thomas et al., 2016; Howlett, 2019). Even the most basic activities of governing such as collecting taxes involves a wide range of issues such as perceptions on the part of taxpayers of the legality and normative "appropriateness" or legitimacy of government's levying and collecting taxes and policy-makers and policy designs need to understand and incorporate these insights and mitigative measures into their designs (March & Olsen, 2004; Malovicki-Yaffe, 2025).

Conclusion: The Need for Better Risk Management

Grappling with the inherent vices of policy-making – unpreparedness, uncertainty, maliciousness, non-compliance, and non-learning – more effectively in the policy sciences would allow a better understanding to emerge of the actual conditions of policy success and failure and the kinds of designs and activities likely to attain government goals in an effective and efficient way, that is, with minimal effort and expenditure. It would also more clearly flag the more volatile efforts that require extensive risk mitigation from those that are more easily handled (Feeley, 1970; Mulford & Etzioni, 1978).

Activities such as non-compliance on the part of policy takers, for example, are key in determining the success of various government initiatives ranging from tobacco control to bus fare evasion (Delbosc & Currie, 2016; Kulick et al., 2016). These behaviors and risks, like those related to uncertainty and maliciousness need to, and can, be accurately "designed for," in the sense that the possibilities of determined non-compliance can be taken into account in a policy design, as can many other similar behaviors, such as free-ridership, fraud and misrepresentation, secrecy and excessive rigidity (Harring, 2016). How these risks can be managed and the experiences of several countries in attempting this are the subjects of the next two sections.

5 A Risk Approach to the Management of Policy Volatility: Adverse Behavior and the Role of Procedural Policy Tools

Introduction: Policy Design and Policy Risks

As this discussion has shown, policy "risk" is a significant issue in policy-making and policy design, but many current studies of these fields underestimate or ignore these challenges. Instead, they rely heavily on assumptions of a more or less riskless policy environment that is absent in real life policy situations. In this section, we take a risk lens to this problem by expanding on the concept of "*volatility*" set out in Section 3, applying it to the design and assessment of policy portfolios in much the same way as financial analysts apply the concept to investment portfolios (Howlett & del Rio, 2016; Rogge & Reichardt, 2016).

Volatility in this sense, as in the financial industry, is a measure of the likelihood or propensity of any design to deploy a set of policy instruments and tools that involve a higher or lower risk of failure. Avoiding or mitigating these risks is an important but understudied aspect of policy-making and thinking about these concerns in terms of hedging against the "inherent" risks outlined in Section 4 is useful in understanding and analyzing them.

Uncertainty, for example, is a risk that is inherent to policy-making because policy-making is forward-thinking and takes place within an uncertain future (Migone and Howlett 2024). And not only are policy solutions subject to uncertainties, but, as we have seen, their formulation, implementation, and evaluation may also be more or less subject to abuses and manipulations that can undermine the ability of a policy design, no matter how clever, to resolve the problems for which it was intended (Howlett, 2019).

As we have seen, such behavior can be found in both policy makers and policy takers (Simon, 1967, 1978; Jones, 2002; Howlett, 2019) and contributes to the enactment or pursuit of bad policy. Policy takers or "targets" may fail to conform with government wishes and rather seek to evade, alter, or "vote with their feet" in ways that undermine even well-intentioned government action. This could be seen recently in the case of the Anti-Vax movement opposing the efforts of public health authorities to increase vaccination rates to protect populations against COVID-19, for example. But it also extends to many other areas, from tax evasion to drug and tobacco use, to automobile speeding and impaired driving where willing compliance with government measures is not automatically forthcoming (Weaver, 2010, 2014, 2015).

As Section 4 highlighted, understanding these sources of policy volatility is important to policy design and to the development of measures intended to correct, offset, or at least mitigate these kinds of risks (Mueller, 2020). Policy designs need to address the possibilities that policy-makers are often "driven by malicious or venal motivations rather than socially beneficial or disinterested ones" (Howlett, 2020b) and that "policy targets also have proclivities towards activities such as gaming, free-ridership and rent-seeking" rather than always obediently complying with government intentions (Howlett, 2020b), as well as the other inherent vices of uncertainty, unpreparedness, and non-learning cited in earlier sections. These are perennial problems not often highlighted in the policy literature but must be curbed if policies are to achieve their aims (Hoppe, 2018; Feldman, 2018; Viscusi & Gayer, 2015).

Reducing Policy Volatility by Design

In the previous section, we had outlined the problems of unpreparedness, uncertainty, maliciousness, non-learning, and non-compliance that contribute to policy volatility. Here we more seriously engage with the need for better policy design-oriented risk assessment to help mitigate these problems and reduce the number of bad policies.

In general, Walker et al. (2013) suggest four principal ways, overlapping to some extent, through which policies can be designed so as to limit their risks of failure. These include designing to enhance:

1) resistance: planning for the worst possible case or future situation and enhancing preparedness;
2) resilience: making sure that the system can recover quickly whatever happens in the future;
3) static robustness: aiming at reducing vulnerability in the largest possible range of conditions; and
4) dynamic robustness (or flexibility): planning to change policies over time, in case conditions change.

But how, precisely, any proposed policies can be assessed and altered or designed to promote and lead to these outcomes is unclear (Howlett and Ramesh 2023).

As is set out later in this section, the kinds of tools or techniques governments have at their disposal to deal with these vices are mainly "procedural" ones. These are tools (Howlett, 2000; Bali et al., 2021) that are put in place to control aspects of policy processes and policy behaviors rather than, as in the case of more substantive tools such as a public enterprise or regulatory commission, to alter the behavior of actors involved in delivering specific kinds of goods and services in society. Like other aspects of policy-making and policy design described earlier, these tools are very important in risk mitigation but are often under-specified and remain under-examined in the mainstream literature on policy tools (Howlett, 2022; Bali et al 2021).

The role these tools can play in risk management and enhance policy designs to promote mitigation is set out here.

Procedural Tools and Risk Management

Procedural policy instruments, unlike their more substantive counterparts, are policy tools or techniques that affect production, consumption, and distribution processes only indirectly (Bali et al., 2021). They are instead concerned with altering aspects of a government's own workings (de Bruijn & ten Heuvelhof,

1997) including its design and risk management activity. Procedural tools do not affect outcomes as directly as substantive tools such as taxes, regulations, sanctions, and levies but are often required for substantive tools, and policy designs, to function effectively.

In many instances these tools have to do with managing actors in the policy process. In the processes of making policy and developing and implementing policy designs, for example, policy actors are arrayed in various kinds of policy networks and just as substantive tools such as regulations can manipulate the actions of citizens and firms in the productive realm, so governments can also manipulate aspects of network policy-making behavior (Howlett & Ramesh, 1998). Thus, for instance, inquiries or commissions can introduce new ideas into an existing network while setting up or making changes to advisory committees can introduce or promote new actors. The behavioral modifications in policy network activity that result from this deployment can affect the articulation of policy goals and means in many ways. In general, however, such tools are "aimed at improving game (policy) interactions and results," but as Klijn, Koppenjan, and Termeer (1995) also note, changes in "networks structure the game without (directly) determining its outcome" (p. 441).

Common examples of procedural policy instruments include, as noted earlier, a government creating a committee of select citizens or experts to aid its policy deliberations and decision-making in contentious areas such as local development or chemical regulation, or establishing public commissions to investigate scandals or accidents (Stark & Yates, 2024). But they also include many other similar tools such as creating citizen juries to decide on key issues such as drug legalization (Smith & Wales, 2000) or the creation of freedom of information legislation, which makes it easier for citizens to gain access to government records, information, and documents and take part in policy deliberations.

These and other similar kinds of procedural tools can also be used in combination with substantive tools to affect governance arrangements in significant ways in the course of public service delivery. For example, the use of networks (Klijn et al., 2015), partnerships (Alford & O'Flynn, 2012), or commissioning and contracting social services (Dickinson et al., 2013; O'Flynn, 2019) can all work together to create a market and designate or alter the range of actors involved in making policy toward it. Internal structural reorganizations can also affect policy processes, as occurs, for example, when natural resource ministries are combined with environmental ones, forcing the two to adopt new operating arrangements affecting policy formulation in ways different from when the two functions are separate (Howlett, 2024).

Table 4 Effects of the use of procedural tools

1. Change actor positions
2. Set down actor positions
3. Add actors
4. Change access rules for actors
5. Influence network formation
6. Promote self-regulation
7. Modify system, e.g. level of market reliance
8. Change evaluative criteria
9. Influence pay-off structure for actors
10. Influence professional and other codes of conduct and behaviour
11. Regulate conflict
12. Change interaction procedures
13. Certify certain types of behaviour
14. Change supervisory relations between actors

Table 4 sets out some of the most common network management activities which procedural policy tools address (Klijn, Koppenian & Termeer, 1995, 2006; Eggers & Goldsmith, 2004).

Procedural instruments included in policy designs can also affect how a policy is formulated and implemented. This includes not only administrative processes and activities for selecting, deploying, and calibrating substantive tools but also those that implement or control policy risks, the main subject of this volume.

As the discussion in earlier sections has shown, studies of these kinds of risks and attempts to mitigate them have shown that a variety of procedural policy tools can and have been used in these efforts. In the case of preparedness, for example, tools such as the preparation of emergency plans, the establishment of agencies to forecast and bring emerging risks to the attention of government have been used, from Centers for Disease Control to central intelligence agencies in the case of national security issues (Lai, 2012). And many similar kinds of tools such as regulatory oversight boards and Comptroller Generals have been used to mandate policy evaluation and attempt to ensure that policy outcomes are carefully monitored and appraised, and appropriate lessons drawn from such evaluations, (Dobell & Zussman, 1981; Dudley, 2020).

The same is true of the other three inherent vices discussed earlier and in this section: uncertainty, maliciousness, and non-compliance.

In the case of uncertainty, the policy volatility it engenders varies across time and is not always manifested in the same way thus requiring different ways to correct. For example, mixes or portfolios of substantive policy tools that rely heavily on markets to produce desired outcomes – such as exists in most countries in areas such

Bad Public Policy 49

as private housing or industrial policy – are always vulnerable to unpredictable swings in market behavior and are thus more highly volatile than public alternatives which are more insulated from price and supply fluctuations (Bode, 2006).

Highly volatile policy areas are often highly resource intensive and require constant monitoring to ensure the public does not suffer from shortages in supply or malicious behavior such as price-gouging. Regulatory or organizationally based policy delivery alternatives, on the other hand, such as a heavily regulated rail transportation system or public housing sectors may require less day-to-day supervision in this sense (Hood, 1983; 1986), although other kinds of long-term uncertainty in matching supply and demand for services outside of market price signals may figure prominently here.

When designing a policy to avoid high levels of non-compliance, as Weaver (2015) has argued, one method governments can employ is to create a "compliance regime" involving a broader mix of tools and elements than is commonly deployed when compliance is considered to be unproblematic. This can include, for example, a major effort to educate the target as to the benefits of compliance and the high costs of non-compliance to themselves, to others or to society as a whole; as occurs with campaigns against littering, smoking, or drug addiction, among others. Designs expected to enhance compliance need to include tools like enhanced public information to provide guidance about what behavior is compliant, how to comply, and the advantages of compliance; often providing admonitions to comply on moral grounds as well as ones related to individual cost-benefit calculations. Governments may also need to provide the resources required for citizens and firms to comply when a policy is targeted to those who would otherwise lack those resources, such as encouraging school attendance in poor countries through Conditional Cash Transfers (CCTs) (Howlett et al 2018). Manipulating options and defaults (choice architecture) in government communications and forms that can encourage certain behavior, like organ donations, without substantially affecting the cost to individuals or governments of complying can also help mitigate this particular vice (Weaver, 2015; Thaler et al 2010).

The general situation with respect to these vices and the kinds of procedural tools that can help address them is set out in Table 5.

Effective policy designs need to include these kinds of procedural tools along with more "substantive" components such as regulations, rules, subsidies, tax incentives, fines, and other such instruments, if the risks to policy effectiveness from the inherent vices of policies are to be lessened.

Of course, a truly malign government may not want to put into place any kinds of arrangements that can restrict its actions, and often the development and implementation of such tools can take place only after the arrival of propitious circumstances, such as following scandal or controversy when

Table 5 Inherent policy risks and management strategies

	Policy Stage/Task	Central Policy Risk	Cause/Source	Management Strategy & Procedural Tools Deployed	Expected Result
	Agenda-Setting	Unpreparedness (Surprise)	Lack of Attention	Institutionalized foresight/Issue Management	Reduced Surprise
	Policy Formulation	Uncertainty (Wickedness)	Lack of Knowledge	Institutionalized Policy Analysis/Risk Management/Modelling	Reduced Ignorance
Sources of Policy Volatility	Decision-Making	Maliciousness (Poor Decisions)	Self-Interestedness	Institutionalized Evidence-Based Policy-Making	Reduced Opportunity for Political or Personal Gain from Poor Decisions
	Policy Implementation	Non-Compliance (Misaligned Target Behavior)	Unknown Behavioral Mechanisms	Institutionalized Policy Design/Policy Labs	Reduced Non-Compliance
	Policy Evaluation	Non-Learning (poor learning)	Unknown Intervention Effects	Institutionalized Evaluation & Measurement	Separates Signal from Noise

a legislature attempts to bind or control the behavior of an executive branch, or when it seeks to create rules and procedures to reduce bureaucratic discretion and ensure administrators remain accountable to elected or appointed officials (Olsen & Peters, 1996; Demonte et al., 2014; Schnell, 2023).

Designing for Portfolio Risk Mitigation: Institutional Mechanisms and Processes

In dealing with risks the policy sciences and policy design literatures can learn not only from financial risk management but from other fields such as industrial engineering and product design, which also have to deal with issues such as mal- or incompetent design and engineering for quick profit or misuse of a product or service by customers.

The Risk Profiles of Policy Portfolios

In financial project portfolio management, for example, rather than attempt to correct each specific risk, often a mix of investments with different risk expectations is created and their risks pooled, with low-risk investments offsetting higher risk ones. This allows portfolios to be calibrated to an investor's risk-return tolerance or preference (Archer & Ghasemzadeh, 1999; Sanchez et al., 2009).

This same kind of "portfolio" logic can be applied to policy-making. That is, policies are generally composed of bundles of policy tools and instruments, and each of these tools and elements is subject to certain kinds of risks in terms of its potential effectiveness (Chapman, 2003; Hennicke, 2004; Milkman, 2012). These "bundles" can be thought of as complex portfolios of tools with each policy tool having a specific risk of failure and the overall portfolio having an aggregate level of volatility. Howlett (2020b) has argued, for example, that "designs based on nodality and nudges and/or treasure resources (e.g. those most closely associated with 'modern' collaborative governance) are always highly volatile as incentives are ripe for cheating and protections are often low (Hood, 1986)". Correctives such as accountability mechanisms, verification and monitoring plans, and the like right can then be added to a design in order to offset these risks (Howlett & Mukherjee, 2019, 2017a).

Controlling Product Quality through Risk Systems

In industries such as manufacturing, techniques for quality control involve similar but different processes involving assigning levels of risk to each aspect of a product and its production that are then managed and minimized. Such processes translate into different steps in different organizations (Aven & Renn, 2010a, 2010b; Burnaby & Hass, 2009; Harvey, 2012; Hopkin, 2018), but "risk management" systems generally go through a cycle of risk identification, assessment, mitigation (or response), and review which are similar to the kinds of analyses undertaken in policy-making and can be emulated in the process of policy design (Persson & Mathiassen, 2009; Hussain et al., 2018).

PriceWaterhouseCoopers, for example, advocate their clients manage risk by creating management systems that assess risk, invoke collaboration between risk and compliance functions in production and then design and review mitigation plans on an annual or other regular basis (PwC, n.d). This is similar to the models proposed by other major accounting and auditing firms. Deloitte, for example, also suggests approaching risk management by creating and institutionalizing a system to (Deloitte, 2009):

- identify risks,
- assess and measure risk,
- respond to those risks,
- design implementing and testing controls, and
- monitor and escalate problems that are observed as the system operates.

Risk assessment systems of this type are commonly used to support decision makers and help them deal with uncertainties in formulation and technological implementation aspects of production processes. Thus, for example, in the aerospace industry and others, the Reliability, Availability, Maintainability, and Safety (RAMS) system (Altavilla & Garbellini, 2002) is used to help identify and quantify risks of failure of all types and has been quite successful in reducing airplane accidents due to mechanical problems. Similarly, Failure Mode Effect and Criticality Analysis (FMECA) is a common risk management tool used in the manufacturing sector that relies on a bottom-up approach to identify common failure modes and assess the consequences (and severity) of component failures for products as a whole.

These kinds of approaches to risk assessment are well suited to policy-making and can accompany more traditional methods of policy analysis (Dunn, 2004) and the design of factors such as the means by which the behavior of administrators and government officials is controlled and activated (McCubbins et al., 1987; Lupia and McCubbins, 1994).

Many countries, of course, do have some form of risk management regime in place that is applied to certain aspects of policy-making processes. However, in most cases these are public safety or national security regimes that deal mainly with external risks such as natural disasters or war or deal with events such as potential exchange rate or commodity price fluctuations. Risk assessment of this type is important and helps deal with some vices such as unpreparedness and uncertainty (Altavilla & Garbellini, 2002). But such techniques also need to be applied to other

Bad Public Policy 53

more "internal" processes and behaviors from learning to compliance which can equally undermine policies and prevent the realization of public value (Rietig, 2019; Dunlop, 2017; Legrand & Vas, 2014; Larsson, 2019). Such efforts have been undertaken, for example, in the creation of conflict of interest legislation, or anti-corruption agencies which can recommend on recruitment, pay and other practices intended to remove opportunities and behaviors which can drive corrupt officials and practices (Quah, 2007; Graycar & Prenzler, 2013; Graycar, 2015).

Conclusion: Designing for Risk

Risk problems are significant for the study and practice of policy design because of the importance they hold for successful policy-making or, to put it another way, due to the implications they have for policy volatility and the propensity and prospects for a policy to fail (McConnell, 2010).

How policy solutions are designed and put into place needs to deal directly both in planning and in implementation with inherent policy risks in addition to risks situated in their external environments that can cause policies to fail (Leong, 2017). Adding a risk management rubric to policy-making and policy design practices can help mitigate the worst potential effects of these risks and inform the use of procedural policy tools needed for their mitigation.

Dealing more seriously in this way with problems around policy volatility and the inherent vices of policy-making is necessary if policy design is to create better and more effective policies. Although the policy sciences lag behind other fields in this area at present, much can be learned from studies and processes found in those other fields, such as engineering and financial product management, but also public administration, accounting, and public management, which have all had to deal directly with the reasons why policies and administrative arrangements fail. Each field has devised a number of means and methods for eliminating or mitigating these risks, and many lessons can be drawn from those efforts for public policy-making including methods and systems for systematically identifying, assessing, and controlling such risks.

In Section 6 the experiences of several prominent countries attempting to put elements of such schemes into practice in policy-making and policy design are discussed.

6 Trends in the Management of Inherent Policy Volatility: Efforts to Manage Internal Policy Risk in Three OECD Countries

Introduction: Internal and External Risks in Policy-Making

Most studies of risk management in government examine only "external" risks such as the impact of climate change, extreme weather events, war or financial calamities on government action, but as the discussion in the previous sections has shown there is a large second area of concern that exists and has received attention in specialized legal, project management, and accountancy circles: that of "internal risks" (Pérez –Morote, 2024). This includes risks inherent to public policy-making related to adverse or malicious behavior of policy makers, to policy "takers" evading or otherwise undermining government initiatives and to factors such as uncertainty, unpreparedness, and non-learning. These inherent risks of bad policies and policy failures are part of the policy world which as argued in the previous section require, but often do not receive, effective treatment in a literature that tends to gloss over many elements of the darkside of public policy-making.

But policy designs need to take this darkside seriously and deal with efforts to mitigate the oft-observed (mis)behavior of policy-makers and the malign, malicious, or venal motivations, which can lead to bad policies as well as mitigate the inherent vices outlined in earlier sections that can also undermine even the most well-intentioned policies.

One example that serves to illustrate the importance of accounting for such risks in policy designs relates to the need in many policies for "truth-telling" on the part of the public. This is an important part of public life and many policies from policing to tax collection rely on members of the public telling the truth about their actions and intentions (Cairney & Wellstead, 2021; Sullivan, 2020). Payment of taxes, honest responses in national census, and, in the recent COVID-19 pandemic, honest and truthful health and vaccination declarations, are all important parts of government action in these areas. The cost of concealed information can be prohibitive for many financial, political, and social policies and outcomes (Bousquet et al., 2019; Teo et al., 2020). Hence, understanding why and under what conditions people behave honestly or maliciously in failing to tell the truth to government is a significant policy problem related to compliance, uncertainty and the risk of policy failure.

Such (mis)behavior must be managed if bad policy outcomes are to be avoided. Ignoring these risks does a disservice to both policy design and policy studies; both these kinds of risks need to be curbed if not eliminated for policies to achieve public value (Feldman, 2018; Hoppe, 2018).

This section reviews three archetypal country-level cases in order to discern the kinds of efforts currently being made in leading countries to manage this side of policy risk: the UK, the US, and Australia. It draws lessons from their recent experiences for how well their policy processes grapple with the management of the "darkside" of policy-making. It proposes a new research agenda dealing with this side of policy-making and urges its incorporation in the work of both scholars and practitioners when they consider many facets of both good and bad policy-making, from policy processes to policy designs and outcomes.

Policy Volatility in Theory and Practice: Internal Threats to Policy Resilience and Robustness

The external risks to policy success stemming from causes such as wars, famines, pandemics, and other kinds of crises are well studied and reasonably well understood (Boin et al., 2005; Boin & 't Hart, 2010). These kinds of risks are the subjects of most current risk management regimes, both in the public and private sector, which focus on monitoring and observing their external environment for signs of financial and other threats to supply chains, product lines, legal liability, and other dynamics that can affect profitability and shareholder value or the attainment of public value and policy expectations (e.g. FATF, 2021; Human Rights Watch, 2021; Pandemic Prevention Institute, 2021).

External risks of this kind are no doubt significant factors affecting policy uncertainty, and their consideration and impact has led to the creation of many policy components and institutions designed to offset this kind of risk. Several of these techniques and strategies have been described in earlier sections, such as foresight agencies and environmental scans and monitoring as well as efforts to enhance government preparedness for problems when they do occur and learning from past efforts and experiences.

Some internal risk factors, such as the potential for fraud, malfeasance, dishonesty, and other actions on the part of government officials and politicians or members of general public, are also recognized and addressed through institutionalized means such as audits and accountancy standards, performance reviews and merit-based hiring, competitive bidding and contracting processes and other kinds of personnel and corporate "best" practices in these areas (Dimand et al., 2024).

A formal classification of all of the kinds of internal risks that governments face, however, is still not available in the literature. Internal risks, for example, are sometimes classified into one or the other of the following types, but this kind of framework does not do justice to all of the many kinds of risks outlined in earlier sections:

(i) *Human-factor risk* – personal factors like strikes, dishonesty, ineffective management by the staff. This type of risk is most relevant at the implementation and administration process of policy-making.
(ii) *Technological or service risks* – technological failure in the process may cause unforeseen interruption in the process.
(iii) *Market risks* – unexpected change in acceptance by the public. This is especially applicable to the process of making decisions and designing policy options (www.investopedia.com/ask/answers/050115/how-can-companies-reduce-internal-and-external-business-risk.asp).

In general, however, what little literature exists on these types of risks is not well linked to that on public policy-making, policy analysis, or policy design, being a feature instead of studies in fields such as public and business management and administration.

Here several facets of these risks that policy-makers and policy designs need to address are set out.

Internal and External Risks in Public Policy Study and Design

As has been argued in earlier sections, both internal and external risks are aspects of policy-making and policy design that together contribute to instability and unpredictability in policy-making and thus critically affect the volatility of a policy. This instability may ultimately lead to policy failure. But, in many cases, these risks can be countered through the use of specific kinds of procedural tools that can help offset some of their most pernicious effects (Howlett, 2020).

In the case of external risks, this often means policy designs may require more redundancy in the form of resources, capabilities, and planning to allow them to deal with potentially emergent crises and problems. Better and stronger efforts to identify and monitor risks such as taking feedback and compiling data allowing adjustment of a policy while it is being implemented, for example, has been suggested as a means through which better designs can emerge and many bad policy outcomes be avoided (Pierson, 1992, 1993; Baumgartner & Jones, 2002; Jacobs & Weaver, 2010).

Importantly, however, such a common-sense approach to managing and mitigating external policy risks runs counter to many currently dominant ideas about effective policy-making and efficient policy designs. The idea that designs should promote or enhance resilience and provide additional resources beyond the minimum, for example, is one often opposed by the desire for more frugal expenditure and distribution of resources in the name of efficiency. The idea of a design calling for continuous adjustments also does not often fit with an emphasis on strict replication of administrative results through the imposition of defined standards and standard operating procedures (Cole & Grossman, 1999; Moxey et al., 1999).

This is also not to say that improved formulation processes surrounding the identification and mitigation of external risks are all that is required for a policy to succeed. As was argued in earlier sections, even if a policy is developed based on best existing theoretical and evidentiary models, it may still fail in practice if it does not address *both* external and internal risks (Nair & Howlett, 2017; Bennett & Lemoine, 2014a, 2014b). This is what is needed to happen even when a policy is exposed to minimal levels of internal risks like fraud, misinterpretation, or dishonesty, as additional resources must be allocated to this area if a design is to function effectively as anticipated (Blanc, 2018).

As we have seen, however, notwithstanding this need, compared to external risks the academic literature has generally been slow to realize the problem of internal policy risks. In many existing cases the purpose of the deployment of procedural tools alongside substantive ones in a policy design is only to slightly enhance the accountability and transparency of governmental action without making a serious contribution to internal risk mitigation (Mergel, 2024; Mergel et al., 2021).

Some governments, however, have attempted to deal with these kinds of risks in a more systematic way and have developed several means through which they can assess and address them. In what follows, the "best practices" found among three leading OECD countries in dealing with or applying risk management models to internal risks (and external) risks are set out.

Models of Policy Risk Management with a Focus on Internal Risks

In a recent study Howlett et al. (2022a and 2022b) examined six countries out of thirty-six OECD member states where English is used as the official language – Ireland, Canada, New Zealand, the US, Australia, and the UK and the efforts they have recently made in the area of internal risk management. Several of these countries did not have a substantial amount of information publicly available on their internal risk management related agencies and procedures (Canada, Ireland, and New Zealand) and were excluded from the final list, leaving Australia, the US and the UK as countries where enough information is publicly available to detail organizational structures, processes, and tools involved in this kind of risk management.

The risk management frameworks followed by these countries is similar to some extent. But important differences also exist. This section sets out the processes and structures uncovered in this study.

The US: An Early Starter but Lately, a Laggard

The US has gone through three distinct phases of development in its risk management efforts, for most of its history focusing mainly on external risks (Moss, 2002). The first phase was during the late 18th and early 19th century when policy-makers mainly focused on identifying and offsetting risks that were thought to potentially negatively affect trade and investment. By the end of 19th century, lawmakers had enacted a wide range of risk management policies, all intended to promote trade and investment. Most notable among them were rules protecting investment and finance such as limited liability, banking regulations, bankruptcy law, a fixed exchange rate, and the predictable enforcement of property rights. These policies help lay the institutional foundation of the American economy.

Phase two started with the dawn of 20th century and brought an entirely new set of external risks to the attention of US policy-makers. These were related to the transition of the country from agriculture to manufacturing and industry. Laws for industrial workers safety, compensation, and unemployment insurance grew substantially, and the nation's social welfare policy for the first time brought the activities of many citizens face to face with the risk management function of the government in the form of welfare payments and unemployment insurance among other elements of the welfare state.

The third phase started in 1960s as the federal government's risk management policy expanded in every area in order to deal with problems such as disasters, the environment, and consumer regulation. In this most recent period, the government also enhanced its risk regime to begin to deal more systematically with internal risk regulation and management. In its current administrative process the US federal government requires each federal agency to comply with a Federal Managers Financial Integrity Act (FMFIA Act) and with Office of Management and Budget (OMB) and Government Accountability Office (GAO) standards for internal control (also called "management control" in OMB documents) of regulations and operations (Hardy, 2010).[1]

The GAO's "Green Book" (GAO, 2014) sets out standards for internal risk management in the federal government and applies to staff at all organizational levels and to all categories of objectives of the organization. It includes reference to International Standard 31000 (ISO, 2018) best practice management procedures, which are expected to provide a common approach to managing any type of risk. This is supplemented with the COSO Enterprise Risk Management (ERM)-Integrated Framework. It first issued in September 2004. It provides a set of risk management standards for businesses of all kinds (COSO, 2004), and was updated in 2017 (COSO, 2017).

These processes help to deal with some potentially malign or malicious administrative behaviors but do little to counter risks related to uncertainty, unpreparedness, or non-learning. And due to their somewhat competing and over-lapping systems, the risk management programs even in their restricted ambit, while extensive, are often limited to specific units and activities or managed on an isolated basis.

---

[1] The GAO's Risk management framework was developed from the Government Auditing Standards, GAO's Green Book, guidance from OMB, work on President's Management Agenda, and the ERM approach of the Committee of Sponsoring Organizations of the Treadway Commission (COSO) (NIST, 2018).

The United Kingdom: Gradual Construction of a Coherent Internal Risk Policy Regime

The situation in the UK has a very different history. A number of regulatory scandals around topics such as Bovine Spongiform Encephalopathy (BSE or mad cow disease) plagued the country at the end of the 20th century and led to increased public distrust of authorities and industry and skepticism concerning the capacity or willingness of the government to manage external risks (Horlick-Jones, 1998; Lofstedt et al., 2011). At the time risk assessment for the regulatory process used to involve mainly closed expert advisory committees which did not meet in public.

These problems led the UK government to initiate a new and more open risk management process to ensure that they "get the balance of regulation right to everyone's benefit" (Department of Trade and Industry, 1993). In 2001 the UK Treasury produced "Management of Risk – A Strategic Overview," known as the Orange Book, and in November 2002, a two-year Risk Program was launched by the Prime Minister in order to drive departments to make risk management more effective and an integral part of their development plans and frameworks. The Orange Book program led to the establishment of a general framework for risk assessment and management expected to be adopted across government.

In support of this program, a report was published by the Prime Minister's Strategy Unit (Prime Minister's Strategy Unit, 2002) about the need for government to recognize that managing both external and internal risk is a key part of its business and set an agenda to improve risk handling(Renn, 2008; National Audit Office, 2004).

Currently the UK Treasury publishes primary references and overviews of good practice for corporate governance in central government departments (generally referred to as "the code") (HM Treasury, 2017 [a]). The current administration process in the UK is structured along textbook principles for risk management systems described in Section 5 (HM Government, 2020). It is a system that focusses on:

1. Risk identification and assessment – how to determine and prioritize how risks should be managed in an organization;
2. Risk Treatment – the selection, design and implementation of risk treatment options in order to support achievement of intended outcomes and manage risks to an acceptable level;
3. Risk Monitoring – the design and operation of integrated risk monitoring; and

4. Risk Reporting – timely, accurate and useful risk reporting is expected to be done to enhance the quality of decision-making and to support the organization in meeting their responsibilities.

With respect to external risks, there is a strong crisis management and emergency planning framework embodying a six-stage process (Plan, Rehearse, Implement, Maintain, Evaluate, and Recover) for responding to external events (Legrand & McConnell, 2012; Government Communication Service, 2018). When it comes to internal risks, in the UK report on Management of Risk (HM Government, 2020), the Treasury notes that there are indeed "inherent risks" that exist in policy and governance and that these require "whole-system-thinking, aligned incentives, positive relationships and collaboration".

But the report also recognizes that the effectiveness of risk management of all kinds depends on the individuals responsible for operating any system to put into place. It also notes that this requires an administrative culture that "embraces openness, supports transparency, welcomes constructive challenge, and promotes collaboration, consultation, and co-operation". It also advises agencies to "invite scrutiny, embrace expertise, and invest in the necessary capabilities and learn from experiences". Policy leads are expected to take explicit steps to involve the public, understand public concerns, and communicate good information about risk.

Treasury codes set out best practices, for example, suggesting that matters of internal risks should be a central focus of an organization's board and also suggests that the boards should be supported by an "audit and risk assurance committee." Such committees are expected to be established in all Executive departments, Non-Departmental Public Bodies, and other agencies. They are expected to undertake the task of internal audit and risk mitigation, working with the External Auditor, and dealing with organization's financial and reporting issues.

Such committees are expected to consist of a suitably experienced non-executive board member (the chair of the committee); an internal audit service (operating to Public Sector Internal Audit Standards); and others. The code mandates that a board's regular agenda should include scrutinizing and advising on risk management and ensuring that such Boards have enough information and resources to efficiently set the organization's risk appetite and ensure a clear framework of governance and risk management exists within each organization.

Unlike the US, then, in the UK some efforts have been made to mitigate some risks related to uncertainty and unpreparedness, in addition to maliciousness, but less so with respect to vices such as non-compliance. And some mechanisms have been put into place to promote learning and mitigate the risk of non-learning. Most of these processes, however, are geared to administrative

Bad Public Policy

behavior rather than policy-making, per se, and their impact on policy designs and policy designing is unclear.

The Commonwealth of Australia: A Fast Learner

In the US, provisions for internal risk management are extensive, but fragmented, and much activity is focused on external risks while the UK has taken some steps to try to unify risk management systems and include both external and some forms of internal risks in its assessments, though largely through an administrative lens.

In Australia, risk management started to be seen as a part of formal governance process only in the 1980s – before this, risk-related matters were only seen as "common sense" prudential management – but the country has caught up quickly to the trends apparent in the US and especially the UK.

As late as the early 1990s, the idea of managing risk systematically throughout an organization was still relatively novel in Australia with most agencies focusing only on specific, mainly financial and insurable, risks. It was becoming increasingly apparent to many in Australian government, however, that a fragmented risk approach, such as that practiced in the US, involving managing risk in silos, did not work well as many risks were found to be highly interdependent.

At that time, an Enterprise Risk Management (ERM) approach started to gain popularity in Australian public management circles. Lam (2000), Deloach (2000), and many other pioneers of the field strongly advocated for ERM and published works outlining how to design and implement an integrated ERM process within a government organization. The adoption of the ERM approach in the Finance Directions to Departments resulted in some early advances in risk management in this area.

The Australian National Audit Office (ANAO) played an important part in this advocacy process through presentations, participation in risk management forums, publications, issuance of Better Practice Guides, and importantly, emphasizing the need to highlight risk management issues in financial statement and performance audits. By the onset of the 21st century, risk assessment and management had been accepted as an essential element of corporate governance and management practice throughout Australian government.

Like the situation in the US and the UK, the current Commonwealth Government policy sets out nine elements required in an agency's Assurance Review Framework (AU. Dept. of Finance, 2017). These are expected to guide the establishment and operation of an appropriate system of risk oversight and management. The central elements required of each department are:

i. Establishing a risk management policy;
ii. Establishing a risk management framework;
iii. Defining responsibility for managing risk;
iv. Embedding systematic risk management into business processes;
v. Developing a positive risk culture;
vi. Communicating and consulting about risk;
vii. Understanding and managing shared risk;
viii. Maintaining risk management capability; and
ix. Reviewing and continuously improving the management of risk.

Much of this work remains centered on external risks. In managing external risks and emergency preparedness, for example, the Australian Government Crisis Management Framework provides for a simple, centralized, and government-wide management scheme. It gives ministers and senior officials guidance on their respective roles and responsibilities in crises and sets out arrangements that link ministers to the work of key officials, committees, and facilities dealing with crises from wildfires to floods and pandemics (AU Dept. of the Prime Minister and Cabinet, 2021).

In managing internal risks Australia takes a unified approach but is mainly limited to managing to mitigate malfeasance and maliciousness. Unlike in the UK and US, Australia's internal risk management system is uniform and evenly distributed throughout each agency's organizational structure. Separate thematic risk assessments are carried out across departments for special topics like security, fraud, and safety, often using specialized accounting and other monitoring methods.

The Commonwealth resource management framework (AU Dept. of Finance, 2019), for example, governs how officials use and manage public resources. The PGPA Act 2013 is the cornerstone of this framework and mandates that the accountable authority must establish and maintain an appropriate system of risk oversight and management, and an appropriate system of internal control to ensure public resources are properly managed.

The Commonwealth Risk Management Policy, published by the Australian federal Department of Finance, sets out the government's expectations for Commonwealth entities in undertaking the business of the government (AU Dept. of Finance, 2014). Under this framework, a "Risk and Internal Control" mandate covers risk management as well as compliance reporting and internal control systems (AU Dept. of Finance, 2020). These tasks include reporting on compliance, fraud control, audit committees, reporting to Joint Committee of Public Accounts and Audit (JCPAA), Model Accountable Authority Instructions, and Australian Government Assurance Reviews. These latter include Implementation Readiness Assessments (IRA), Gateway Reviews Processes, and Assurance Reviews Processes.

Analysis: Internal Risk Management in Practice

This review of three leading OECD countries shows that while external risks are now commonly considered and monitored on an extensive and systematic basis, only limited progress has been made toward the recognition and management of internal or inherent policy risks outside of risks of fraud and corruption. And in some countries like the US this is done in an *ad hoc* and decentralized way.

In the UK, risk assessment in general only recently became a matter of governmental concern after high public attention due to a series of high profile policy failures (Dunlop, 2017). Most innovations happened during the first decade of the 21st century, when major transformations in UK risk management took place (Grant, 2009). These include developing risk assessment as an integral part of government policies and for public companies that were also required to implement risk policies and disclose their risk data. Audit and risk committees in the UK are now important entities in government organizations.

The corporate governance structure of internal risk management in US, on the other hand, is highly focused on internal control and financing, and risk management in this area is a joint function of the department's financial officer, office of Inspector General and staff, along with guidelines from OMB's Circular, GAO's Green Book, and other programs. The result is a patchwork of risk assessment and management processes. Agencies nevertheless generally follow the Government Performance and Results (GPRA) and the GPRA Modernization Act (GPRAMA) and produce annual performance reports to report their strategies, goals, and operations to the Congress. Currently, however, many agencies do not (and are not required to) have an independent risk management framework.

The internal risk management system in the Australian government on the other hand is the most uniform of the three countries. Today, risk assessment is part of all levels of governance in Australian agencies and includes both external and some internal risk management. Throughout the corporate structure, risk management regulations are strongly embedded, and responsibilities are assigned to every layer of government. As in the UK, audit committees are the most important mechanism for internal risk assessment and are comprised of board members, executive board members, and independent members.

Table 6 outlines the risk management processes found in the three jurisdictions.

Table 6 Risk management process in US, UK, and Australia compared

Risk Management Processes	US' Risk Management Structure	UK's Risk Management Structure	Australia's Risk Management Structure
Risk identification	• Control Environment	• Risk identification and assessment	• Establishing the risk management policy • Establishing risk management framework • Defining responsibilities • Embedding risk management into business processes and systems
Assessment	• Risk Assessment		• Developing a positive risk culture • Establishing communication and consultation about organization's risk
Mitigation	• Control Activities • Information and Communication	• Risk Treatment	• Understanding and managing shared risk • Maintaining risk management capability
Review	• Monitoring	• Risk Monitoring • Risk Reporting	• Reviewing and continuously improving the management of risk

While this situation is an improvement on earlier eras, these systems remain limited and restricted in scope, with a primary emphasis on monitoring and mitigating external risks and only very partial application to some internal risks, namely maliciousness and unpreparedness. Important areas of policy volatility, including compliance, uncertainty and learning remain very much under-represented.

Conclusion: Existing Risk Management Regimes and Their Principal Focus on External Risk

Policy volatility or the propensity for policies to fail is affected by both external and internal factors, although in both the scholarly literature and governmental practice most attention has been paid in the past to, and continues to be lavished upon, the former.

Bad policy actions, however, can result from the personal enrichment of proponents, and policy-making can be gamed and governments defrauded or may be unprepared for changes in their environments and crises (Howlett, 2020), and the risk management systems of leading OECD countries try to deal with some of the most pernicious and important aspects of these vices. But other aspects of poor policy processes and outcomes have only been studied systematically on rare occasions and are generally overlooked in existing government policies and procedures for risk management.

Nevertheless, as the three case studies show, some governments have begun to create guidelines and agencies to systematically anticipate and mitigate some of these kinds of internal risks. Such risk management is vital if a government is to meet its goals. Without better internal risk management, it is difficult to offset policy risks once a program or policy is in place (Falco, 2017; Taylor et al., 2019). The comparison of the risk management processes of the three countries set out earlier shows that some efforts have been made in leading OECD countries to deal with some of these issues proactively. The processes in the US and the UK, however, are still very broad and do not establish as clear links to the managing internal risks as occurs in Australia, and still deal mainly with the need for enhanced preparedness to meet external crises.

As a result of this neglect, in most countries policy designs continue to be developed with only the most rudimentary and cursory knowledge of the kinds of "internal" policy risks they face. There remains a pressing need to "design in" correctives beyond stricter financial accountability mechanisms, verification, and monitoring. Dealing with the inherent risks or policies and policy-making requires a specific set of mitigative procedural tools to be fully developed and implemented in order to offset the risks of failure posed to policy designs and policy activity.

7 Conclusion: Vigilance and Vices

There is a darkside to public policy that is manifested in bad policy outcomes and bad policies. It is found where the separate or combined vices of uncertainties, poor preparation, poor competencies, or the ill-intent of actors or groups of actors thwart the ability of policies to serve the public interest. It includes both the activities of policy makers and policy takers, and this behavior needs to be carefully examined and incorporated into thinking about policy-making if it is to advance the creation of effective policy designs (Howlett, 2021).

To anyone who has worked in public policy, the challenges of complexity, ambiguity, and error are familiar and unwelcome companions in policy formulation, decision-making, and implementation. The five inherent vices of policy identified here – unpreparedness, non-learning, uncertainty, maliciousness, and non-compliance – remain a constant threat to policy-makers. These sources of policy volatility inhere naturally in processes of administering vast and sprawling state institutions, processes, and infrastructure, and the possibility of policy failure from them is an ever-present threat.

Vices Revisited

Our intention here has been to focus attention upon two sources and meanings of bad policies: normative analyses of what is meant by serving the public interest and the negative effects of replacing it with the private, and more technical analysis of the nature of the "inherent vices" or the built-in problems of policy-making that can easily generate bad or poorly performing policies.

The former aspect of bad policies was discussed in the early sections of the book in terms of the norms of democratic and liberal democratic governments and the assumptions about the meaning of good government that adhere to the policy sciences. Attention was paid to their origin in liberal democratic precepts and the pressures those assumptions face in the contemporary era due to counter-currents such as populism and democratic backsliding. The second aspect was discussed in terms of five problems that adhere to policy processes and require dedicated action to be overcome or at least their effects mitigated.

Unpreparedness is always an issue as circumstances change in sometimes difficult to predict ways. *Uncertainty* arises from "ill-structured" or "wicked" problems where solutions are elusive but also exists well beyond that in terms of scope and intractability. *Maliciousness* refers to the vulnerability of government and public policies to manipulation by self-interested actors. *Non-compliance* represents a key barrier to effective policy implementation, including not just administrative challenges but also intentional resistance or circumvention of government intent by target populations. And *non-learning* is also always a problem as evaluating policy effort and outcomes and the links between them is highly challenging.

While some of these inherent vices have received attention from both practitioners and scholars, others have not. Problems around uncertainty and unpreparedness, for example, especially in the context of external risks, have led to the creation of risk assessment systems in government which try to also control some problems with maliciousness such as corruption and malfeasance. The role of malice in policy-making, however, is a key subject in policy-making, which has been given scant attention in the field notwithstanding its extensive analysis in other cognate fields such as law, political science or public administration. From boardrooms to the ballot boxes, a variety of actors – from decision-makers and administrators, to implementing agents and the intended beneficiaries of policies – can endeavor to distort public processes for personal or electoral gain, and this well-known penchant needs to be addressed directly in public policy studies. Learning is also a subject which has received a great deal of attention along with its variants such as poor or non-learning.

These kinds of vices are not merely of scholarly interest as they have practical, palpable consequences for the real quality of government as it is encountered by citizens on the ground. Malice and maliciousness, for example, manifest themselves in a range of behaviors that are bad for policy: the use of public authority to favor particular ethnic or religious groups, or to penalize sections of the public for, perhaps, voting for a different party, or belonging to an unfavored region. They might even include policy-makers making profit for themselves, via companies in which they have a financial interest or through much more direct forms of bribery, corruption, and self-aggrandizement.

Compliance is another such issue that has not received its due attention. Existing governmental risk identification and management systems do not cover it, and research in implementation studies has been committed to scrutinizing administrative behavior and its pitfalls, from principal-agent chains to financial and human resource constraints, rather than the equally important issue of compliance. As was noted by Weaver (2009) above, target population compliance is very much "the final frontier" of implementation research. Policy success is intrinsically dependent on the behavior of those they aim to influence – the "policy takers" – and more effort is needed to both study this vice and design for it.

Compliance is a good example of a vice that requires in-depth analysis. It is not merely a matter of blithe or blind rule-following: public compliance, in liberal democracies and elsewhere, is a matter of consent. To consider policy targets as "static entities," as some perspectives from the 1970s and 1980s have held, is myopic. The public are neither inert nor infinitely malleable, and their behavior is shaped by a myriad of factors, from levels of trust and social norms to their perception of the government's legitimacy in even a addressing an issue in the first place.

As we have suggested in this Element, orthodox accounts of policy compliance focus on calibrating incentives and disincentives to "steer" targets toward desirable behavior. Such approaches sidestep the social and political questions of who gets to be a "target," and minimize the intricate behaviors that lead to both non-compliance and compliance.

A better approach for dealing with this vice, by contrast, is one which more actively seeks to account for the multifaceted and often somewhat unpredictable behaviors of the targets – crucial in myriad sectors, from littering to traffic safety. Anticipating and mitigating such behavior entails not just tackling determined non-compliance through better research but also pre-empting such behavior. Recent years has seen an uptick in scholarly interest in the subject, leading to the rise of what has been called the "behavioral turn" in the discipline as more attention has been turned to understanding policy-taker motivations (Leong & Howlett, 2019). This is a promising development in advancing the agenda of research into the darkside of policy-making and bad policy.

The Need for Vigilance

These behaviors and others linked to policy vices enhance the *uncertainties* inherent in policy-making and in doing so augment policy volatility and the chances of policy failure. While risks are often thought to concern mainly the risk of adverse exogenous events, many cases of bad policy involve deviations from the public good and the attainment of public value that occur through a lack of effective organizational processes for internal risk assessment. As such, they potentially can be curtailed through improved internal risk regulatory mechanisms and processes ranging from more robust policing and anti-corruption agencies to checks and balances in contracting, expenditure, and recruitment.

Developing more robust and effective internal risk management policies, however, requires policy advisors, analysts, and decision-makers to recognize, manage, and strategize for these variegated vices, necessitating policy designs that are not just agile and flexible, as required in navigating the "normal wickedness" encountered in policy-making, but also resilient in turbulent environments where policy landscapes shift quickly.

There is some evidence that these concerns for better risk management and the acknowledgment of inherent vices and the dark-side of policy-making are being recognized by some governments and a set of procedural tools developed and deployed to deal with some of them. But as the discussion of the UK, US, and Australian cases earlier has shown, this record of policy initiatives has been focused on OECD governments and even there has been uneven.

It is, nevertheless, the task of the vigilant and ethical policy professional in government, as well as those working in policy analysis and policy design practice, to identify and diminish these vices to the fullest extent possible. Doing so is fundamental to ensuring that democratic governance is properly maintained and, perhaps just as importantly, seen to be maintained.

The values of good government are threatened where policy is misaligned with the public interest, whether bad policy emerges through poor policy design; obscured by murky decision-making methods; or its outcomes subverted by the ulterior political or private agendas of bad faith actors. The central conception of Fritz Scharpf's (2003) framing of legitimacy is that the essence of democratic governance lies in its ability to align the will of the public with governmental actions, while Luetjens, Mintrom, and t'Hart have also contended that political legitimacy in public policy is dependent on *both* the outcomes and the methods used in aligning of policies with systemic governance values (2019, p. 5).

That is, the legitimacy of public policy is not merely an abstraction but a socially sanctioned political obligation to make good governmental decisions. As a result, there is no straightforward process for dealing with the darkside for two reasons: first, there is a multilayered mediation of public will expressed through institutional structures, electoral systems, and other mechanisms in every country and each of these are imperfect. At best they are akin to a palimpsest or impressionist reflections of a general public will, but this "impression" is often all that an administrative apparatus has to go on as the final executor of the public's will. And second, the nature of policy risks is that they are omnipresent and the "default" in any policy-making situation. Conscious, dedicated, and well-informed action is needed, continuously, for their mitigation.

Giving Light to the Darkness

Formulating a policy that mobilizes available state resources to achieve government aims is bedeviled by the complex social, economic, environmental, and political circumstances in which state managers and policy professionals are only partially sighted navigators. The "causal theory" of a public policy – "if we want to achieve x, then we need to do y and z – usually has countless confounding or countervailing variables.

However, a key part of the problem with the presence of bad policy has been the scholarly neglect of policy risks, and especially "internal" ones, and a lack of attention to steps that can be taken to deal with them. While the "procedural" tools needed to mitigate policy vices are well-understood in the fields of public administration and anti-corruption studies, among others, policy studies as a discipline has yet to fully assimilate them into its core frameworks (Bali et al., 2021; Lang, 2019).

Our framing of bad policy as a normative and analytical possibility in this short work is no more than a beachhead for policy scientists working on and against the "darkside" of public policy. Extant scholarship provides foundational understandings of the subject, such as the literature cited in this Element, but leaves considerable scope for further research that can more comprehensively guide policy formulation, implementation, and design. Future studies need to integrate these disparate strands of knowledge to offer non-Panglossian solutions to the complicated and often negative realities of policy-making.

In synthesizing the insights from existing works on the subject, our work calls for a more nuanced understanding of bad public policy – one that integrates the crucial role of the public in conferring legitimacy, warns against the dangers posed by policy vices for policy failure, and guards against intentional divergence from the public interest. Such a comprehensive perspective is not merely an academic exercise but an empirical one too: an urgent imperative for preserving the ethos, quality, and effectiveness of public policy.

The relationship between democratic expression, state-administered outcomes, and the subsequent legitimacy of public policy is not easily established, and it is quite clear that a failure of alignment between these three elements does not necessarily reveal the presence of bad faith political actors (Peter and Nagel 2025). That said, it is our view that many policy scholars have neglected to consider the circumstances in which bad actors can misappropriate public institutions, their resources, and powers and create bad policy. Drawing attention to the risk that the public interest and the achievement of public value can be easily undermined by the vices *inherent* to policy processes is, as we have argued, an urgent undertaking for analysts who have often modelled public policy processes on the assumption that institutions are populated by political actors operating in good faith and kept well in check by well-functioning institutional safeguards when these both may be sorely lacking.

These risk problems are significant for the study and practice of policy-making and policy design due to the implications they have for policy volatility and how likely it is for a policy to fail and why (McConnell, 2010). That government intentions may be ill-informed, and state and governance knowledge bases and capacities limited, that decisions may not solely be oriented toward the creation of public value; and that policy targets may indulge in various forms of "misconduct" from fraud to gamesmanship, undermining government intentions of whatever kind – all these are only very rarely, if ever, examined in the policy design

Bad Public Policy 71

literature despite their prevalence in other fields of scholarly attention and inquiry (Arestis & Kitromilides, 2010; Howlett, 2020, 2021).

Dealing more seriously with these problems around policy volatility and inherent vices is necessary if policy design is to achieve its purpose of creating better and more effective policies. What we call for is the incorporation of redundancies and adaptive mechanisms that allow for effective monitoring and mid-course corrections, a theme echoed in the works of Pierson (1992), among others. This can be done through a variety of means – from institutionalizing foresight agencies to deal with the risk of surprises affecting government agendas to improving and mainstreaming evaluation and measurement activities to reduce the risk of poor or non-learning occurring in policy evaluation (Dudley & Xie, 2022; Dudley, 2022).

Although the policy sciences lag behind in this area at present, much can be learned from studies in other fields, which have had to deal more often and more directly with the reasons why the artifacts they produce often fail. The new focus on policy-maker and policy-taker behavior that has already been noted in works on the "behavioral turn" (Leong, 2020), for example, holds out much hope in shedding light on the causes and origins of bad policy and how it can be avoided.

In undertaking this analysis, the Element explicitly seeks to re-center the normative components of public policy analysis and policy design work to re-emphasize the place of the public interest and legitimacy in state institutions and the role they play in the creation of good policies, and the avoidance of bad policy and poor outcomes. That is, what has often been thought to be "good" policy-making has an explicit, values-based dimension, and the identification of these values, which may or may not exist in any given country, is an important component of identifying the sources of policy volatility and its correctives.

To tackle this challenge, we have, in this Element, proposed an analysis of the "darkside" and possible corrective measures that equips scholars and policy-makers alike with, first, the certainty that this is indeed a topic of vital importance to all public policy enterprises – from research and analysis to design and implementation – second, a sense of the kinds of tools and techniques that can be deployed to offset or mitigate these problems, and third, a "set of concepts" – policy volatility, inherent vices and policy risks – which can help gain purchase into these phenomena.

The Element thus offers a method to help give form and "light" to the "darkness." Looking at policies as a portfolio of risks, analogous to what is done with investment portfolios in the case of the financial industry, where a portfolio logic is used to deal with the uncertainties involved in market forecasting and investment packages are tailored to specific risk preferences of consumers and investors, is a helpful heuristic in this effort (McFarlan, 1981;

Archer & Ghasemzadeh, 1999; Pellegrinelli, 1997; Olsson, 2008; Project Management Institute, 2008; Sanchez et al., 2008; Sanchez, et al., 2009; Teller & Kock, 2013). And so are as are the systems for risk management developed by businesses and industry. The insights from these models and systems can help inform policy design thinking. Minimizing volatility and mitigating the internal risks of policy-making should be undertaken with this logic in mind.

The Element invites policy-makers, scholars, and the public to engage more thoughtfully with the ideas of good governance and the public interest in policy-making, considering them not as self-evident terms but rather as concepts requiring ongoing and public interpretation and negotiation. As we have mentioned several times in this Element, there is no necessary link between bad policy and regime type. Bad policies exist in liberal democratic countries as well as authoritarian and other types and this point should not be forgotten.

We contend that a rigorous understanding of policy volatility, inherent vices, and internal risk mitigation is necessary for the vitality and sustainability of good governance and effective public policy. Our attention to "inherent vices" is also a call to vigilance. Policy-making is a complex and challenging endeavor plagued by uncertainty, susceptible to manipulation, and often undermined by non-compliance. Effective policy-making and the avoidance of bad policies requires explicit strategies for addressing these issues and necessitates a multi-disciplinary, multi-tool approach. Such an approach goes well beyond the findings and works of the traditional literature on policy success and failure found in the historical and recent policy sciences and is a subject well worth pursuing in more detail in all its ramifications.

References

Albertazzi, D., and D. McDonnell. *Populists in Power*. London: Routledge, 2015.

Alford, J. L., and J. O'Flynn. *Rethinking Public Service Delivery*. England: Palgrave Macmillan, 2012.

Altavilla, A., and L. Garbellini. "Risk Assessment in the Aerospace Industry." *Safety Science* 40, no. 1 (February 1, 2002): 271–98.

Alvarez, S. E., Dagnino, E., and Escobar, A. "Introduction: The Cultural and the Political in Latin American Social Movements." In S. E. Alvarez, E. Dagnino, and A. Escobar (Eds.), *Cultures of Politics of Cultures* (pp. 1–30). New York: Routledge.

Anderson, C. W. *Statecraft: An Introduction to Political Choice and Judgement*. New York: John Wiley and Sons, 1977.

Archer, N. P., and F. Ghasemzadeh. "An Integrated Framework for Project Portfolio Selection." *International Journal of Project Management* 17, no. 4 (1999): 207–16.

Arestis, P., and Y. Kitromilides. "What Economists Should Know about Public Policymaking?" *International Journal of Public Policy* 6, no. 1/2 (2010): 136–53.

AU Dept. if the Prime Minister and Cabinet. Australian Government Crisis Management Framework, 2021. https://pmc.gov.au/sites/default/files/publications/aus-gov-crisis-management-framework-v3-0.pdf.

AU Dept. of Finance. Commonwealth Risk Management Policy, 2014. www.finance.gov.au/sites/default/files/2019-11/commonwealth-risk-management-policy_0.pdf.

AU Dept. of Finance. Implementing the Commonwealth Risk Management Policy (RMG 211), 2020. Managing Commonwealth Resces, www.finance.gov.au/government/managing-commonwealth-resces/implementing-commonwealth-risk-management-policy-rmg-211.

AU Dept. of Finance. Managing Commonwealth Resces, 2019. www.finance.gov.au/government/managing-commonwealth-resces.

AU. Dept. of Finance. Australian Government Assurance Reviews – Rescue Management Guide No. 106, 2017.

Aven, T., & O. Renn. "Risk Management." In T. Aven and O. Renn (Eds.), *Risk Management and Governance* (pp. 121–58). Berlin: Springer, 2010a.

Aven, T., & O. Renn. *Risk Management and Governance: Concepts, Guidelines and Applications* (Vol. 16). Heidelberg: Springer Science & Business Media, 2010b.

Bächtold, S. "The Smartphone and the Coup: How Myanmar's Conflicts are Entangled with Digital Technologies, Policies and Violence." *International Journal of Public Policy*, 16, no. 5–6 (2022): 293–310.

Baldwin, D. A. *Economic Statecraft*. Princeton, NJ: Princeton University Press, 1985.

Bali, A. S., M. Howlett, J. Lewis, & M. Ramesh. "Procedural Policy Tools in Theory and Practice." *Policy & Society* 40, no. 3 (2021): 295–311.

Bamberg, S., and G. Möser. "Twenty Years after Hines, Hungerford, and Tomera: A New Meta-Analysis of Psycho-Social Determinants of Pro-environmental Behaviour." *Journal of Environmental Psychology* 27, no. 1 (March 2007): 14–25.

Barile, L., J. Cullis, and P. Jones. "Will One Size Fit All? Incentives Designed to Nurture Prosocial Behaviour." *Journal of Behavioral and Experimental Economics* 57 (August 2015): 9–16.

Bason, C. *Design for Policy*. Farnham: Gower Pub Co, 2014.

Bason, C., and R. D. Austin. "Design in the Public Sector: Toward a Human Centred Model of Public Governance." *Public Management Review* (June 9, 2021): 1–31.

Bauer, M. W., and C. Knill. "A Conceptual Framework for the Comparative Analysis of Policy Change: Measurement, Explanation and Strategies of Policy Dismantling." *Journal of Comparative Policy Analysis: Research and Practice* 16, no. 1 (2014): 28–44.

Baumgartner, F. R., and B. D. Jones. "Positive and Negative Feedback in Politics." In F. R. Baumgartner and B. D. Jones (Eds.), *Policy Dynamics* (pp. 3–28). Chicago: University of Chicago Press, 2002.

Bell, D. A., D. Brown, K. Jayasuriya, and D. M. Jones. *Towards Illiberal Democracy in Pacific Asia* (Vol. 193). London: Palgrave Macmillan UK, 1995.

Bendor, J., K. Sunil, and S. A. David. "Satisficing: A 'Pretty Good' Heuristic." *The B.E. Journal of Theoretical Economics* 9, no. 1 (2009): 1–38.

Bennett, N., and G. J. Lemoine. "What a Difference a Word Makes: Understanding Threats to Performance in a VUCA World." *Business Horizons* 57, no. 3 (May 1, 2014b): 311–17.

Bennett, N., and J. Lemoine. "What VUCA Really Means for You." *Harvard Business Review* 92, no. 1/2 (2014a).

Bigo, D. "Security, Exception, Ban and Surveillance." In *Theorizing Surveillance* (pp. 60–82). Abingdon: Willan, 2006.

Birkland, T., and S. Waterman. "Is Federalism the Reason for Policy Failure in Hurricane Katrina?" *Publius: The Journal of Federalism* 38, no. 4 (2008): 692–714.

Bitonti, A. "Where It All Starts: Lobbying, Democracy and the Public Interest." *Journal of Public Affairs* 20, no. 2 (2020): e2001.

Blanc, F. *From Chasing Violations to Managing Risks: Origins, Challenges and Evolutions in Regulatory Inspections*. Cheltenham: Edward Elgar, 2018.

Bobrow, D. "Policy Design: Ubiquitous, Necessary and Difficult." In B. Guy Peters and J. Pierre (Eds.), *Handbook of Public Policy* (pp. 75–96). London: SAGE, 2006.

Bobrow, D. B., and J. S. Dryzek. *Policy Analysis by Design*. Pittsburgh: University of Pittsburgh Press, 1987.

Bode, I. "Disorganized Welfare Mixes: Voluntary Agencies and New Governance Regimes in Western Europe." *Journal of European Social Policy* 16, no. 4 (2006): 346–59.

Boin, A. *Governing after Crisis: The Politics Of Investigation, Accountability and Learning*. Cambridge: Cambridge University Press, 2008.

Boin, A., and P. 't Hart. "Organising for Effective Emergency Management: Lessons from Research1." *Australian Journal of Public Administration* 69, no. 4 (2010): 357–71.

Boin, A., P. 't Hart, E. Stern, and B. Sundelius. *The Politics of Crisis Management: Public Leadership under Pressure*. Cambridge: Cambridge University Press, 2005.

Botterill, L. C., and A. Fenna. *Interrogating Public Policy Theory: A Political Values Perspective*. Glos, UK: Edward Elgar Publishing, 2019.

Bousquet, L., G. Poniatowski, C. Vellutini, and G. Casamatta. *Estimating International Tax Evasion by Individuals*. Luxembourg : Publications Office of the European Union, 2019.

Braithwaite, V. A., ed. *Taxing Democracy: Understanding Tax Avoidance and Evasion*. Aldershot, Hants, England: Ashgate Pub, 2003.

Brancati, D. "Democratic Authoritarianism: Origins and Effects." *Annual Review of Political Science* 17, no. 1 (2014): 313–26.

Bredenhoff-Bijlsma, R. "Policy Development under Uncertainty: A Framework Inspired by Cases of Water Management. Enschede, the Netherlands: Gildeprint, 2010.

Breunig, C., and C. Koski. "Interest Groups and Policy Volatility." *Governance* 31, no. 2 (2018): 279–97.

Brik, A. B., and L. A. Pal, eds. *The Future of the Policy Sciences*. New Horizons in Public Policy. Cheltenham, UK: Edward Elgar Publishing, 2021.

Broadbent, J. "Comparative Climate Change Policy Networks." In J. N. Victor, A. H. Montgomery, and M. Lubell (Eds.), *The Oxford Handbook of Political Networks* (pp. 875–900). New York: Oxford University Press, 2016.

Burnaby, P., and S. Hass, S. "Ten Steps to Enterprise–Wide Risk Management." *Corporate Governance: The International Journal of Business in Society* 9, no. 5 (2009): 539–50.

Busenberg, G. "Wildfire Management in the United States: The Evolution of a Policy Failure." *Review of Policy Research* 21, no. 2 (2004): 145–56.

Cairney, P., and A. Wellstead. "COVID-19: Effective Policymaking Depends on Trust in Experts, Politicians, and the Public." *Policy Design and Practice* 4, no. 1 (2021): 1–14.

Cameron, M. "From 'Queue Jumpers' to 'Absolute Scum of the Earth': Refugee and Organised Criminal Deviance in Australian Asylum Policy." *The Australian Journal of Politics and History* 59, no. 2 (2013): 241–59.

Cameron, B. T., and B. Evans. "Policy Capacity Research: An Overview and Bibliography of the International Literature, 1978 to 2023." *International Review of Public Policy* 6, no. 1 (April 1, 2024): 110–41.

Capano, G., and J. Jie Woo. "Resilience and Robustness in Policy Design: A Critical Appraisal." *Policy Sciences* 37, no. 4 (2018): 422–40.

Capano, G., M. Howlett, D. S. L. Jarvis, M. Ramesh, and N. Goyal. "Mobilizing Policy (In)Capacity to Fight COVID-19: Understanding Variations in State Responses." *Policy and Society* 39, no. 3 (July 3, 2020): 1–24.

Carothers, T., and A. O'Donohue, eds. *Democracies Divided: The Global Challenge of Political Polarization*. Washington, DC: Brookings Institution Press, 2019.

Cappella, J. N., and K. H. Jamieson. "News Frames, Political Cynicism, and Media Cynicism." *The Annals of the American Academy of Political and Social Science* 546 (1996): 71–84.

Chapman, R. "A Policy Mix for Environmentally Sustainable Development – Learning from the Dutch Experience." *New Zealand Journal of Environmental Law* 7, no. 1 (2003): 29–51.

Chapman, G., K. L. Milkman, D. Rand, T. Rogers, and R. H. Thaler. "Nudges and Choice Architecture in Organizations: New Frontiers." *Organizational Behavior and Human Decision Processes* 163 (2021): 1–3.

Chindarkar, N., M. Howlett, and M. Ramesh. "Conceptualizing Effective Social Policy Design: Design Spaces and Capacity Challenges." *Public Administration and Development* 37, no. 1 (February 1, 2017): 3–14.

Churchman, C. W. "Wicked Problems." *Management Science* 14, no. 4 (1967): B141–42.

Clarke, D. M. *Journalism and Political Exclusion: Social Conditions of News Production and Reception*. Montreal: McGill-Queen's Press, 2014.

Cohen, M. D., J. G. March, and J. P. Olsen. "People, Problems, Solutions and the Ambiguity of Relevance." In J. G. March and J. P. Olsen (Eds.), *Ambiguity and Choice in Organizations* (pp. 24–37). Bergen: Universitetsforlaget, 1979.

Cole, D. H., and P. Z. Grossman. "When Is Command-and-Control Efficient – Institutions, Technology, and the Comparative Efficiency of Alternative Regulatory Regimes for Environmental Protection." *Scholarship and Professional Work - Business* 28 (1999): 887–938.

Colebatch, H. K. "The Idea of Policy Design: Intention, Process, Outcome, Meaning and Validity." *Public Policy and Administration* 33, no. 4 (October 1, 2018): 365–83.

Colebatch, H. K. *Policy*. Minneapolis: University of Minnesota Press, 1998

Colebatch, H. K. "Valuing Public Value: Recognising and Applying Knowledge about the Governmental Process." *Australian Journal of Public Administration* 69, no. 1 (2010): 66–78.

Compton, M. E., J. Luetjens, and P. t'Hart. "Designing for Policy Success." *International Review of Public Policy* 1, no. 1:2 (October 10, 2019): 119–46.

COSO. Enterprise Risk Management – Integrated Framework, 2004. www.coso.org/Pages/erm-integratedframework.aspx.

COSO. Guidance on Enterprise Risk Management, 2017. www.coso.org/Pages/erm.aspx.

Cousins, B. "Design Thinking: Organizational Learning in VUCA Environments." *Academy of Strategic Management Journal* 17, no. 2 (2018): 1–18.

Cox, T. "Muddling-Through and Deep Learning for Managing Large-Scale Uncertain Risks." *Journal of Benefit-Cost Analysis* 10, no. 2 (2019): 226–50.

Crowley, K., J. Stewart, A. Kay, and B. Head. *Reconsidering Policy: Complexity, Governance and the State*. 1st ed. Bristol, UK: Bristol University Press, 2020.

Dahlström, C., J. Lindvall, and B. Rothstein. "Corruption, Bureaucratic Failure and Social Policy Priorities." *Political Studies* 61, no. 3 (2012): 523–42.

Dalacoura, K. "Islamist Terrorism and the Middle East Democratic Deficit: Political Exclusion, Repression and the Causes of Extremism." *Democratization* 13, no. 3 (2006): 508–25.

Damonte, A., C. A. Dunlop, and C. M. Radaelli. "Controlling Bureaucracies with Fire Alarms: Policy Instruments and Cross-Country Patterns." *Journal of European Public Policy* 21, no. 9 (October 21, 2014): 1330–49.

De Bruijn, J. A., and E. F. Ten Heuvelhof. "Instruments for Network Management." In *Managing Complex Networks: Strategies for the Public Sector* (pp. 119–36). London: SAGE Publications Ltd., 1997.

De Goede, M. "Proscription's Futures." *Terrorism and Political Violence* 30, no. 2 (2018): 336–55.

De Montis, A., A. Ledda, and S. Caschili. "Overcoming Implementation Barriers: A Method for Designing Strategic Environmental Assessment Guidelines." *Environmental Impact Assessment Review* 61 (November 2016): 78–87.

Delbosc, A., and G. Currie. "Four Types of Fare Evasion: A Qualitative Study from Melbourne, Australia." *Transportation Research Part F: Traffic Psychology and Behaviour* 43, no. 4 (November 1, 2016): 254–64.

DeLeon, P. Reinventing the policy sciences: Three steps back to the future. *Policy Sciences* 27, no. 1 (1994): 77–95.

Deloach, J. *An Executive Summary of Enterprise-Wide Risk Management – Strategies for Linking Risk and Opportunity.* London: Financial Times Prentice Hall, 2000.

DeLoach, J. W. *Enterprise-Wide Risk Management.* London: Prentice-Hall, 2000.

Deloitte. Take the Right Steps – 9 Principles for Building the Risk Intelligent Enterprise, 2009. in-gc-putting-risk-in-the-comfort-zone-nine-principles-for-risk-intelligent-enterprises-noexp.pdf.

Denny, E. S., and P. Zittoun, eds. *Handbook of Teaching Public Policy.* Northampton: Edward Elgar Publishing, 2024.

Department of Trade and Industry. (1993). Regulation in the Balance: a Guide to Risk Assessment Department. London: Department of Trade and Industry.

Dewey, J. *The Public and Its Problems.* 3rd ed. Chicago: Swallow Press, 1954.

Dickinson, H., J. Glasby, A. Nicholds, and H. Sullivan. "Making Sense of Joint Commissioning: Three Discourses of Prevention, Empowerment and Efficiency." *BMC Health Services Research* 13, no. 1 (2013): S6.

Dimand, A.-M., A. S. Patrucco, S. Abutabenjeh, and B. M. Brunjes. "Insights Into Public Procurement: Principles, Processes, and Partnership Dynamics." In *Reference Module in Social Sciences.* Amsterdam: Elsevier, 2024. https://doi.org/10.1016/B978-0-443-13701-3.00350-9.

Diamond, L., and L. Morlino. "The Quality of Democracy: An Overview." *Journal of Democracy* 15, no. 4 (2004): 20–31.

Dobell, R., and D. Zussman. "An Evaluation System for Government: If Politics Is Theatre, Then Evaluation Is (Mostly) Art." *Canadian Public Administration* 24, no. 3 (1981): 404–27.

Dodge, J., L. Elgert, and R. Paul. "On the Social Relevance of Critical Policy Studies in Times of Turmoil." *Critical Policy Studies* 16, no. 2 (2022): 131–32.

Doig, A., and S. Johnson. "New Public Management, Old Populism and the Policing of Fraud." *Public Policy and Administration* 16, no. 1 (2001): 91–111.

Douglas, S., T. Schillemans, P. 't Hart, et al. "Rising to Ostrom's Challenge: An Invitation to Walk on the Bright Side of Public Governance and Public Service." *Policy Design & Practice* 4, no. 4 (December 2021): 441–51.

Dowling, M. E., and T. Legrand. "'I Do Not Consent': Political Legitimacy, Misinformation, and the Compliance Challenge in Australia's Covid-19 Policy Response." *Policy and Society* 42, no. 3 (2023): 319–33.

Dryzek, J. S. "A Post-Positivist Policy-Analytic Travelogue." *The Good Society* 11, no. 1 (2002): 32–36.

Dryzek, J. S. "Policy Analysis as Critique." In M. Moran, M. Rein, and R. E. Goodin (Eds.), *The Oxford Handbook of Public Policy*, 190–204. New York: Oxford University Press, 2008.

Dryzek, J. S. "Policy Sciences of Democracy." *Polity* 22, no. 1 (1989): 97–118.

Dudley, S. E. "The Office of Information and Regulatory Affairs and the Durability of Regulatory Oversight in the United States." *Regulation & Governance* 16, no. 1 (2022): 243–60.

Dudley, S. E., and Z. Xie. "Designing a Choice Architecture for Regulators." *Public Administration Review* 80, no. 1 (2020): 151–56.

Dudley, S. E., and Z. Xie. "Nudging the Nudger: Toward a Choice Architecture for Regulators." *Regulation & Governance* 16, no. 1 (2022): 261–73.

Dunleavy, P. *Theories of the State: The Politics of Liberal Democracy*. London: Macmillan International Higher Education, 1987.

Dunlop, C. A. "Pathologies of Policy Learning: What Are They and How Do They Contribute to Policy Failure?" *Policy & Politics* 45, no. 1 (2017): 19–37.

Dunn, W. *Public Policy Analysis: An Introduction*. Upper Saddle River: Pearson/Prentice Hall, 2004.

Dunn, W. N. *Public Policy Analysis*. 6th ed. London: Routledge, 2017.

Durnová, A. P., and Weible, C. M. "Tempest in a Teapot? Toward New Collaborations between Mainstream Policy Process Studies and Interpretive Policy Studies." *Policy Sciences* 53, no. 3 (2020): 571–88.

Dye, T. R. *Understanding Public Policy*. Englewood Cliffs: Prentice-Hall, 1972.

Edelman, M. J. *Constructing the Political Spectacle*. Chicago: University of Chicago Press, 1988.

Eggers, W. D., and S. Goldsmith. *Government by Network: The New Public Management Imperative*. Deloitte Research/Ash Institute for Democratic Governance and Innovation at the John F. Kennedy School of Government at Harvard University, 2004.

Eijlander, P. "Possibilities and Constraints in the Use of Self-Regulation and Co-Regulation in Legislative Policy: Experiences in the Netherlands—Lessons to Be Learned for the EU." *Electronic Journal of Comparative Law* 9, no. 1 (2005): 1–8.

Ellig, J., and D. Lavoie. "The Principle-Agent Relationship in Organizations." In P. Foss (Ed.), *Economic Approaches to Organizations and Institutions : An Introduction* (pp. 267–95). Aldershot: Dartmouth, 1995.

Falco, G. Constraint Tree Analysis: A Method to Evaluate Threats to Technology Policy Goals. *SSRN Scholarly Paper*. Rochester: Social Science Research Network, 2017. https://papers.ssrn.com/abstract=2939209.

Farr, J., J. S. Hacker, and N. Kazee, N. (2006). "The Policy Scientist of Democracy: The Discipline of Harold D. Lasswell." *American Political Science Review* 100, no. 4 (2006): 579–87.

FATF. (2021) Guidance on Proliferation Financing Risk Assessment and Mitigation. www.fatf-gafi.org/publications/financingofproliferation/documents/proliferation-financing-risk-assessment-mitigation.html.

Feeley, M. "Coercion and Compliance: A New Look at an Old Problem." *Law & Society Review* 4, no. 4 (May 1, 1970): 505–19.

Feldman, Y. *The Law of Good People: Challenging States' Ability to Regulate Human Behavior*. 1 ed. New York: Cambridge University Press, 2018.

Field, S. L. "What's in a Name? How a Democracy Becomes an Aristocracy," 2016. https://core.ac.uk/display/365180298?utm_source=pdf&utm_medium=banner&utm_campaign=pdf-decoration-v1.

Fischer, F. *Politics, Values, and Public Policy: The Problem of Methodology*. Boulder, CO: Westview Press, 1980.

Fischer, F. *Technocracy and the Politics of Expertise*. London: Sage, 1990.

Franchino, F., and B. Hoyland. "Legislative Involvement in Parliamentary Systems: Opportunities, Conflict and Institutional Constraints." *American Political Science Review* 103, no. 4 (2009): 607–21.

Friedman, L. S. *The Microeconomics of Public Policy*. Princeton: Princeton University Press, 2002.

Fukuyama, F. "Capitalism & Democracy: The Missing Link." *Journal of Democracy* 3, no. 3 (1992): 100–10.

Gans-Morse, J., S. Mazzuca, and S. Nichter. "Varieties of Clientelism: Machine Politics during Elections." *American Journal of Political Science* 58, no. 2 (April 1, 2014): 415–32.

GAO. (2014). Standards for Internal Control in the Federal Government. GAO-14-704G. www.gao.gov/assets/gao-14-704g.pdf.

Gelber, K., 2011. *Speech Matters: Getting Free Speech Right*. University of Queensland Press.

Gelber, K., and M. McDonald. Ethics and Exclusion: Representations of Sovereignty in Australia's Approach to Asylum-Seekers. *Review of International Studies* 32, no. 2 (2006): 269–89.

Goetz, A. M. "Manouevring Past Clientelism: Institutions and Incentives to Generate Constituencies in Support of Governance Reforms." *Commonwealth and Comparative Politics* 45, no. 4 (2007): 403–24.

Goggin, M. L. *Policy Design and the Politics of Implementation: The Case of Child Health Care in the American States.* Knoxville: University of Tennessee Press, 1987.

Goldhamer, H. *The Adviser.* New York: Elsevier, 1978.

Goodin, R. E. *Manipulatory Politics.* New Haven: Yale University Press, 1980.

Goodin, R. E., ed. *The Oxford Handbook of Political Science.* Oxford: OUP Oxford, 2009.

Goodin, R. E., M. Rein, and M. Moran. "The Public and Its Policies." In M. Moran, M. Rein, and R. E. Goodin (Eds.), *The Oxford Handbook of Public Policy.* New York: Oxford University Press, 2006.

Government Communication Service. (2018). Emergency Planning Framework. https://3x7ip91ron4ju9ehf2unqrm1-wpengine.netdna-ssl.com/wp-content/uploads/2020/04/Emergency-planning-framework-1.pdf.

Grant, W. "Intractable Policy Failure: The Case of Bovine TB and Badgers." *British Journal of Politics and International Relations* 11 (2009): 557–73.

Graycar, A. "Corruption: Classification and Analysis." *Policy and Society* 34, no. 2 (June 1, 2015): 87–96.

Graycar, A., and T. Prenzler. *Understanding and Preventing Corruption.* 2013 ed. London: Palgrave Pivot, 2013.

Habermas, J. *Knowledge and Human Interests.* Boston: Beacon Press, 1974.

Hacker, J. S. "Policy Drift: The Hidden Politics of US Welfare State Retrenchment. In W. Streeck and K. Thelen (Eds.), *Beyond Continuity: Institutional Change in Advanced Political Economies* (pp. 40–82). Oxford: Oxford University Press, 2005.

Hallsworth. Policy Making in the Real World *Evidence and Analysis,* 2010.

Hallsworth, M., and J. Rutter. *Making Policy Better: Improving Whitehall's Core Business.* London: The Institute for Government, 2011. www.instituteforgovernment.org.uk/our-work/better-policy-making/making-policy-better.

Hansson, S. O. "Decision Making under Great Uncertainty." *Philosophy of the Social Sciences* 26 (1996): 369.

Hansson, S. "Defensive Semiotic Strategies in Government: A Multimodal Study of Blame Avoidance." *Social Semiotics* 28, no. 4 (August 8, 2018): 472–93.

Hardy, K. Managing Risk in Government: An Introduction to Enterprise Risk Management. IBM Center for the Business of Government. http://enterrasolutions.com/media/docs/2013/09/RiskinGovernment.pdf, 2010.

Harring, N. "Reward or Punish? Understanding Preferences toward Economic or Regulatory Instruments in a Cross-National Perspective." *Political Studies* 64, no. 3 (October 1, 2016): 573–92.

Harvey, G. E. "The Process of Risk Management: Important Steps to Take." *Petroleum Accounting and Financial Management Journal* 31, no. 1 (2012): 77.

Hawkins, K., and J. M. Thomas, eds. *Making Regulatory Policy*. Pittsburgh: University of Pittsburgh Press, 1989.

Head, B. "Reconsidering Evidence-Based Policy: Key Issues and Challenges." *Policy and Society* 29, no. 2 (2010): 77.

Head, B. "Three Lenses of Evidence-based Policy." *Australian Journal of Public Administration* 67, no. 1 (2008b): 1–11.

Head, B. "Wicked Problems in Public Policy." *Public Policy* 3, no. 2 (2008a): 101–18.

Hennicke, P. "Scenarios for a Robust Policy Mix: The Final Report of the German Study Commission on Sustainable Energy Supply." *Energy Policy* 32, no. 15 (October 2004): 1673–78.

Herzog, B. "Invisibilization and Silencing as an Ethical and Sociological Challenge." *Social Epistemology* 32, no. 1 (January 2, 2018): 13–23.

Hibbing, J. R., and E. Theiss-Morse. *Stealth Democracy: Americans' Beliefs about How Government Should Work*. New York: Cambridge University Press, 2002.

Hinterleitner, M. *Policy Controversies and Political Blame Games*. Cambridge Studies in Comparative Public Policy. Cambridge: Cambridge University Press, 2020.

Hinterleitner, M. "Policy Failures, Blame Games and Changes to Policy Practice." *Journal of Public Policy* 38, no. 2 (June 2018): 221–42.

Hirschman, A. O. *The Passions and the Interests: Political Arguments for Capitalism before Its Triumph*. Princeton: Princeton University Press, 1977.

HM Government. (2020). The Orange Book – Management of Risk – Principles and Concepts. London: HM Government. https://assets.publishing.service .gov.uk/government/uploads/system/uploads/attachment_data/file/866117/ 6.6266_HMT_Orange_Book_Update_v6_WEB.PDF.

HM Treasury. *Audit and Risk Assurance Committee handbook*. London: HM Treasury, 2016. Retrieved September 10, 2020, https://assets.publishing .service.gov.uk/government/uploads/system/uploads/attachment_data/file/ 512760/PU1934_Audit_committee_handbook.pdf.

HM Treasury. Corporate Governance in Central Government Departments: Code of Good Practice. London: HM Treasury, 2017a. https://assets.publish ing.service.gov.uk/government/uploads/system/uploads/attachment_data/ file/609903/PU2077_code_of_practice_2017.pdf.

HM Treasury. Guidance Code of Conduct for Board Members of Public Bodies, June 2019. September 10, 2020, www.gov.uk/government/publications/code-of-conduct-for-board-members-of-public-bodies/code-of-conduct-for-board-members-of-public-bodies-june-2019.

Hood, C. *The Blame Game: Spin, Bureaucracy, and Self-Preservation in Government*. Princeton, NJ: Princeton University Press, 2010.

Hood, C. *The Tools of Government*. Chatham: Chatham House, 1986.

Hood, C. "Using Bureaucracy Sparingly." *Public Administration* 61, no. 2 (1983): 197–208.

Hopkin, P. *Fundamentals of Risk Management: Understanding, Evaluating and Implementing Effective Risk Management*. London: Kogan Page, 2018.

Hoppe, R. "Heuristics for Practitioners of Policy Design: Rules-of-Thumb for Structuring Unstructured Problems." *Public Policy and Administration* 33, no. 4 (October 1, 2018): 384–408.

Horlick-Jones, T. "Meaning and Contextualisation in Risk Assessment." *Reliability Engineering and System Safety* 59 (1998): 79–89.

Howard, M. M. "The Impact of the Far Right on Citizenship Policy in Europe: Explaining Continuity and Change." *Journal of Ethnic and Migration Studies* 36, no. 5 (2010): 735–51.

Howlett, M. "Avoiding a Panglossian Policy Science: The Need to Deal with the Darkside of Policy-Maker and Policy-Taker Behaviour." *Public Integrity* 24, no. 3 (May 4, 2022): 306–18.

Howlett, M. "Challenges in Applying Design Thinking to Public Policy: Dealing with the Varieties of Policy Formulation and Their Vicissitudes." *Policy & Politics* 48, no. 1 (2020a): 49–65.

Howlett, M. "Dealing with the Dark Side of Policy-Making: Corruption, Malfeasance and the Volatility of Policy Mixes." In A. Graycar (Ed.), *Handbook on Corruption, Ethics and Integrity in Public Administration* (pp. 67–79). Cheltenham: Edward Elgar, 2020b.

Howlett, M. "Dealing with the Dark Side of Policy-Making: Managing Behavioural Risk and Volatility in Policy Designs." *Journal of Comparative Policy Analysis: Research and Practice* 22, no. 6 (2020): 612–25.

Howlett, M. *Designing Public Policies: Principles and Instruments*. 2nd ed. London: Routledge, 2019.

Howlett, M. *Designing Public Policies: Principles and Instruments*. London: Routledge, 2024.

Howlett, M. "Managing the 'Hollow State': Procedural Policy Instruments and Modern Governance." *Canadian Public Administration* 43, no. 4 (2000): 412–31.

Howlett, M. "Matching Policy Tools and Their Targets: Beyond Nudges and Utility Maximisation in Policy Design." *Policy & Politics* 46, no. 1 (January 18, 2018): 101–24.

Howlett, M. "The Lessons of Failure: Learning and Blame Avoidance in Public Policy-Making." *International Political Science Review* 33, no. 5 (2012): 539–55.

Howlett, M., ed. *The Routledge Handbook of Policy Tools*. New York: Routledge, 2022.

Howlett, M. "Volatility in Policy Mixes: A Research Agenda." Paper Presented to the International Conference on Public Policy, Montreal, 2019.

Howlett, M., and C. Leong. "Policy Volatility and the Propensity of Policies to Fail: Dealing with Uncertainty, Maliciousness and Compliance in Public Policy-Making." *International Journal of Public Policy* 16, no. 5/6 (2022): 236–52.

Howlett, M., and C. Leong. "The 'Inherent Vices' of Policy Design: Uncertainty, Maliciousness, and Noncompliance." *Risk Analysis* 42, no. 5 (2022): 920–30.

Howlett, M., and C. Leong. "What Is Behavioral in Policy Studies? How Far Has the Discipline Moved Beyond Traditional Utilitarianism?" *Journal of Behavioral Public Administration* 5, no. 1 (April 14, 2022): 1–21.

Howlett, M., and D. Jarvis. "Policy Science beyond Self-Congratulatory Virtue Signaling: Matching Supply and Demand in the Scholarship, Pedagogy and Purpose of the Policy Enterprise." In A. Brik and L. Pal (Eds.), *The Future of the Policy Sciences* (pp. 51–69). Cheltenham, UK: Edward Elgar, 2021.

Howlett, M., and I. Mukherjee. "Design and Non-Design in Policy Formulation: Where Knowledge Meets Power in the Policy Process." In I. Mukherjee (Ed.), *Handbook of Policy Formulation* (pp. 1–23). Cheltenham: Edward Elgar, 2017.

Howlett, M., and I. Mukherjee, eds. *Handbook of Policy Formulation*. Cheltenham: Edward Elgar, 2017a.

Howlett, M., and I. Mukherjee. *Handbook of Policy Design*. New York: Routledge, 2019.

Howlett, M., and M. Ramesh. "Achilles' Heels of Governance: Critical Capacity Deficits and Their Role in Governance Failures." *Regulation & Governance* 10, no. 4 (2016): 301–13.

Howlett, M., and M. Ramesh. "Policy Subsystem Configurations and Policy Change: Operationalizing the Postpositivist Analysis of the Politics of the Policy Process." *Policy Studies Journal* 26, no. 3 (1998): 466–82.

Howlett, M., & Ramesh, M. *Studying Public Policy: Policy Cycles and Policy Subsystems*. Oxford: Oxford University Press, 2003.

Howlett, M., and P. del Rio. "The Parameters of Policy Portfolios: Verticality and Horizontality in Design Spaces and Their Consequences for Policy Mix Formulation." *Environment and Planning C* 33, no. 5 (2015): 1233–45.

Howlett, M., and S. Nair. "The Central Conundrums of Policy Formulation: Ill-Structured Problems and Uncertainty." In I. Mukherjee (Ed.), *Handbook of Policy Formulation* (pp. 23–38), Cheltenham, UK: Edward Elgar Publishing, 2017.

Howlett, M., and T. LeGrand. "Advancing the Study of the Concepts of Policy Risk and Malignancy." *International Journal of Public Policy* 16, no. 5/6 (2022): 227–35.

Howlett, M., C. Leong, and S. Sahu. "Managing Internal Policy Risk: Australia, the UK and the US Compared." *Policy Design and Practice* 5, no. 2 (April 21, 2022a): 1–12.

Howlett, M., S. Sahu, and C. Leong. "Trends in the Management of Policy Volatility: Managing Internal Policy Risk in Three OECD Countries." *International Journal of Public Policy* 16, no. 5/6 (2022b): 345–61.

Howlett, M., M. Ramesh, and G. Capano. "Policy-Makers, Policy-Takers and Policy Tools: Dealing with Behaviourial Issues in Policy Design." *Journal of Comparative Policy Analysis: Research and Practice* 22, no. 6 (November 1, 2020): 487–97.

Howlett, Michael, and M. Ramesh. "Designing for Adaptation: Static and Dynamic Robustness in Policy-making." *Public Administration* 101, no. 1 (March 2023): 23–35. https://doi.org/10.1111/padm.12849.

Howlett, Michael, M. Ramesh, and Kidjie Saguin. "Diffusion of CCTs from Latin America to Asia: The Philippine 4Ps Case." *Revista de Administração Pública* 52 (April 2018): 264–84. https://doi.org/10.1590/0034-761220170020.

Huber, J. D., and G. B. Powell. "Congruence between Citizens and Policymakers in Two Visions of Liberal Democracy." *World Politics* 46, no. 3 (1994): 291–326.

Hueso, A., and Bell, B. "An Untold Story of Policy Failure: The Total Sanitation Campaign in India." *Water Policy* 15, no. 6 (2013): 1001–17.

Human Rights Watch. (2021). World Report 2021. Human Rights Watch. www.hrw.org/world-report/2021.

Hussain, K., & W. Khan, and J. Z. Khan. . Job Safety Analysis and Risk Assessment a Case Study of Frontier Ceramics Ltd, 2018. www.researchgate.net/profile/Zahid-Hussain-5/publication/328723240_Job_Safety_Analysis_and_Risk_Assessment_A_case_study_of_Frontier_Ceramics_Ltd/links/5bddb05da6fdcc3a8dbb3e67/Job-Safety-Analysis-and-Risk-Assessment-A-case-study-of-Frontier-Ceramics-Ltd.pdf.

Ingram, H., and A. Schneider. "Improving Implementation through Framing Smarter Statutes." *Journal of Public Policy* 10, no. 1 (1990): 67–88.
Ingram, H. and S. R. Smith, eds. *Public Policy for Democracy*. Washington, DC: Brookings Institution Press, 2011.
ISO. ISO 31000:2018 Risk Management Guidelines, 2018. ISO 31000:2018: www.iso.org/obp/ui#iso:std:iso:31000:ed-2:v1:en.
Jacobs, A. M., and R. K. Weaver. "When Policies Undo Themselves: Self-undermining Feedback as a Source of Policy Change. *Governance* 28, no. 4 (2015): 441–57.
Jacobs, A., and R. Weaver. Policy Feedback and Policy Change. SSRN Scholarly Paper. Rochester: Social Science Research Network, 2010.
Jarvis, L., and T. Legrand. "The Proscription or Listing of Terrorist Organisations: Understanding, Assessment, and International Comparisons." *Terrorism and Political Violence* 30, no. 2 (March 4, 2018): 199–215.
Jensen, O. "Climate Risk Perceptions and Policy Ambition." *International Journal of Public Policy* 16, no. 2–4 (January 2022): 151–73.
Jones, B. D. "Bounded Rationality and Public Policy: Herbert A. Simon and the Decisional Foundation of Collective Choice." *Policy Sciences* 35 (2002): 269–84.
Jordan and Adelle. Environmental Policy in the EU. Actors, Institutions and Processes. Routledge. ISBN: 1849714681, 9781849714686, 2012.
Jordan, A., and E. Matt. "Designing Policies That Intentionally Stick: Policy Feedback in a Changing Climate." *Policy Sciences* 47, no. 3 (September 2014): 227–47.
Karp, P. (2016). Tony Abbott Says Europe Is Facing "Peaceful Invasion" of Asylum Seekers. *The Guardian*, 2016. www.theguardian.com/australia-news/2016/sep/19/tony-abbott-says-europe-is-facing-peaceful-invasion-of-asylum-seekers.
Kiss, B., C. G. Manchón, and L. Neij. "The Role of Policy Instruments in Supporting the Development of Mineral Wool Insulation in Germany, Sweden, and the United Kingdom." *Journal of Cleaner Production* 48 (2013): 187–99.
Kleiman, M. A. R, and S. M. Teles. "Market and Non-market Failures." In M. Moran, M. Rein, and R. E. Goodin (Eds.), *The Oxford Handbook of Public Policy* (pp. 624–50). Oxford: Oxford University Press, 2008.
Klijn, E. H., and J. F. Koppenjan. "Institutional Design: Changing Institutional Features of Networks." *Public Management Review* 8, no. 1 (2006): 141–60.
Klijn, E. H., J. Koppenjan, and K. Termeer. "Managing Networks in the Public Sector: A Theoretical Study of Management Strategies in Policy Networks." *Public Administration* 73, no. 3 (1995): 437–54.

Klijn, E. H., T. Ysa, V. Sierra, E. Berman, J. Edelenbos, and D. Y. Chen. "The Influence of Network Management and Complexity on Network Performance in Taiwan, Spain and the Netherlands." *Public Management Review* 17, no. 5 (2015): 736–64.

Knight, F. H. *Risk, Uncertainty, and Profit*. Boston: Houghton Mifflin Company, 1921.

Koppenjan, J., and E. H. Klijn. 2004. *Managing Uncertainties in Networks: A Network Approach to Problem Solving and Decision Making*. New York: Routledge.

Krasteva, A. "Editorial of Special Focus: Securitisation and Its Impact on Human Rights and Human Security." *Global Campus Human Rights Journal* 3 15–22.

Krasteva, A. "Re/De/constructing Far-Right Youth: Between the Lost Generation and Contestatory Citizenship." In G. Lazaridis and G. Campani (Eds.), *Understanding the Populist Shift: Othering in a Europe in Crisis*, (pp. 150–78). New York: Routledge, 2017.

Kuhn, M., and L. Siciliani. "Manipulation and Auditing of Public Sector Contracts." *European Journal of Political Economy* 32 (2013): 251–67.

Kulick, J., J. Prieger, and M. A. R. Kleiman. "Unintended Consequences of Cigarette Prohibition, Regulation, and Taxation." *International Journal of Law, Crime and Justice* 46 (September 1, 2016): 69–85.

Lai, A. Y. "Organizational Collaborative Capacity in Fighting Pandemic Crises: A Literature Review from the Public Management Perspective." *Asia Pacific Journal of Public Health* 24, no. 1 (2012): 7–20.

Lam, J. "*Enterprise-Wide Risk Management and the Role of the Chief Risk Officer*." White paper, March 25, 2000, London: ERisk, pp. 1–5.

Lang, A. "Collaborative Governance in Health and Technology Policy: The Use and Effects of Procedural Policy Instruments." *Administration & Society* 51, no. 2 (2019): 272–98.

Larsson, A., L. Ekenberg, A. Paulsson, and M. Danielson. "Tool Development for Risk Management Decisions under Strong Uncertainty." *AGU Fall Meeting Abstracts* 21 (December 1, 2019). http://adsabs.harvard.edu/abs/2019AGUFMPA21B1128L.

Lasswell, H. D. "From Fragmentation to Configuration." *Policy Sciences* 2, no. 4 (December 1971): 439–46.

Lasswell, H. D. *National Security and Individual Freedom*. New York: McGraw-Hill, 1950.

Lasswell, H. D. "The Policy Orientation." In D. Lerner and H. D. Lasswell (Eds.), *The Policy Sciences: Recent Developments in Scope and Method* (pp. 3–15). Stanford: Stanford University Press, 1951.

Lasswell, H. D. *Who Gets What, When, How*. New York: Whittlesey House, 1936.

Laurie, M., and Petchesky, R. P. "Gender, Health, and Human Rights in Sites of Political Exclusion." *Global Public Health* 3, no. S1 (2008): 25–41.

Lee, S., and M. J. Moon. "Managing Policy Risks Using Big Data Analytics in the Pandemic Era: VUCA and Wicked Policy Problems." *International Journal of Public Policy* 16, no. 5–6 (2022): 362–78.

Legrand, T. *The Architecture of Policy Transfer.* Cham: Springer International Publishing, 2021.

Legrand, T. *The Architecture of Policy Transfer: Ideas, Institutions and Networks in Transnational Policymaking.* Cham: Palgrave Macmillan, 2020.

Legrand, T. "The Malign System in Policy Studies: Strategies of Structural and Agential Political Exclusion." *International Journal of Public Policy* 16, no. 2–4 (2022): 88–105.

Legrand, T., and L. Jarvis. "Enemies of the State: Proscription Powers and Their Use in the United Kingdom." *British Politics* 9, no. 4 (December 1, 2014): 450–71.

Legrand, T., and A. McConnell. "Conclusion: Issues for the Future: Emerging Debates on the Intersection of Globalisation and National Crisis Management." In T. Legrand and A. McConnell (Eds.), *Emergency Policy Volume III* (pp. 493–500). 1st ed. United Kingdom: Ashgate Publishing Limited, 2012.

Legrand, T., and C. Vas. "Framing the Policy Analysis of OECD and Australian VET Interaction: Two Heuristics of Policy Transfer." *Journal of Comparative Policy Analysis: Research and Practice* 16, no. 3 (2014): 230–48.

Leigh, A. "Thinking Ahead: Strategic Foresight and Government." *Australian Journal of Public Administration* 62, no. 2 (2003): 3–10.

Leong, C. "Hajer's Institutional Void and Legitimacy without Polity." *Policy Sciences*, 50 (2017): 573–83.

Leong, C. "Narratives of Sanitation: Motivating Toilet Use in India." *Geoforum* 111 (2020): 24–38.

Leong, C., and M. Howlett. "Policy Learning, Policy Failure, and the Mitigation of Policy Risks: Re-Thinking the Lessons of Policy Success and Failure." *Administration & Society* 54, no. 7 (August 1, 2022): 1379–401.

Leong, C., and M. Howlett. "The 'Inherent Vices' of Policy Design: Uncertainty, Maliciousness and Non-Compliance." *Risk Analysis* 42, no. 5 (2022): 920–30.

Levin, S. A. "Public Goods in Relation to Competition, Cooperation, and Spite." *Proceedings of the National Academy of Sciences* 111, supplement 3 (2014): 10838–45.

Levin, K., B. Cashore, S. Bernstein, and G. Auld. "Overcoming the Tragedy of Super Wicked Problems: Constraining Our Future Selves to Ameliorate Global Climate Change." *Policy Sciences* 45, no. 2 (2012): 123–52.

Linder, S. H., and B. G. Peters. "Research Perspectives on the Design of Public Policy: Implementation, Formulation, and Design." In D. J. Palumbo and D. J. Calista (Eds.), *Implementation and the Policy Process: Opening up the Black Box* (pp. 51–66). New York: Greenwood Press, 1990.

Linder, S. H., and B. G. Peters. "The Analysis of Design or the Design of Analysis?" *Policy Studies Review* 7, no. 4 (1988): 738–50.

Lippmann, W. *Public Opinion*. New York: Macmillan, 1946.

Lofstedt, R., F. Bouder, J. Wardman, and S. Chakraborty. "The Changing Nature of Communication and Regulation of Risk in Europe." *Journal of Risk Research* 14, no. 4 (2011): 409–29.

Luetjens, J., M. Mintrom, and P. t'Hart. *Successful Public Policy: Lessons from Australia and New Zealand*. Canberra: ANU Press, 2019.

Lupia, A., and McCubbins, M. D. "Learning from Oversight: Fire Alarms and Police Patrols Reconstructed." *Journal of Law, Economics and Organization* 10, no. 1 (1994): 96–125.

MacDonald, F. "Positioning Young Refugees in Australia: Media Discourse and Social Exclusion." *International Journal of Inclusive Education* 21, no. 11 (2017): 1182–95.

Machiavelli, N. *The Prince*. Edited by Quentin Skinner and Russell Price. New York: Cambridge University Press, 1988.

Maddison, S. "Evidence and Contestation in the Indigenous Policy Domain: Voice, Ideology and Institutional Inequality." *Australian Journal of Public Administration* 71, no. 3 (2012): 269–77.

Maiden, S. Former PM Tony Abbott warns IS Terrorists Are Hiding in Flood of Refugees, *The Daily Telegraph*, 2015. www.dailytelegraph.com.au/news/nsw/former-pm-tony-abbott-warns-is-terrorists-are-hiding-in-flood-of-refugees/news-story/5404f8ab654370dfe7a081cf83d99ec9.

Manor, J. "Post-Clientelist Initiatives." In T. M. Shaw (Ed.), *Democratization in the Global South* (pp. 243–53). International Political Economy. London: Palgrave Macmillan, 2013.

Manski, C. F. "Policy Analysis with Incredible Certitude." *The Economic Journal* 121, no. 554 (August 1, 2011): F261–89.

Manski, C. F. *Public Policy in an Uncertain World: Analysis and Decisions*. Cambridge, MA: Harvard University Press, 2013.

March, J. G., and J. P. Olsen. "The Logic of Appropriateness." Oslo: ARENA, ARENA Working Paper 9, 2004.

Marion, J., and E. Muehlegger. "Measuring Illegal Activity and the Effects of Regulatory Innovation: A Study of Diesel Fuel Tax Evasion." Faculty Research Working Paper Series RWP07-026, John F. Kennedy School of Government, Harvard University, Cambridge, MA, May 2007.

Malovicki-Yaffe, Nechumi, Boaz Hameiri, Leah Bloy, and Ram Fishman. "Environmental Taxation Triggers Persistent Psychological Resistance to Climate Policy." *Policy Sciences* 58 (2025). https://doi.org/10.1007/s11077-025-09565-w.

Mathijssen, J., A. Petersen, P. Besseling, A. Rahman, and H. Don. Dealing with Uncertainty in Policymaking. CPB/PBL/Rand Europe, 2008.

Maxim, L., and van der Sluijs, P. Jereon. "Quality in Environmental Science for Policy: Assessing Uncertainty as a Component of Policy Analysis." *Environmental Science and Policy* 14 (2011): 482–92.

McConnell, A. "Hidden Agendas: Shining a Light on the Dark Side of Public Policy." *Journal of European Public Policy* 25, no. 12 (2018): 1739–58.

McConnell, A. "Policy Success, Policy Failure and Grey Areas In-Between." *Journal of Public Policy* 30, no. 03 (2010): 345–62.

McConnell, A. "Rethinking Wicked Problems as Political Problems and Policy Problems." *Policy & Politics* 46, no. 1 (January 18, 2018): 165–80.

McConnell, A. *Understanding Policy Success: Rethinking Public Policy.* Basingstoke: Palgrave Macmillan, 2010.

McConnell, A., and A. Stark. "Bureaucratic Failure and the UK's Lack of Preparedness for Foot and Mouth Disease." *Public Policy and Administration* 17, no. 4 (2002): 39–54.

McConnell, A., and T. Legrand. *Emergency Policy: Volume III.* London: Routledge, 2017.

McCubbins, M. D., R. G. Noll, and B. R. Weingast. "Administrative Procedures as Instruments of Political Control." *Journal of Law, Economics, and Organization* 3, no. 2 (1987): 243–77.

McDonald, M. "Deliberation and Resecuritization: Australia, Asylum-Seekers and the Normative Limits of the Copenhagen School." *Australian Journal of Political Science* 46, no. 2 (2011): 281–95.

McFarlan, F. W. "Portfolio Approach toInformation Systems." *Harvard Business Review* 59 no. 5 (1981): 142–50.

Mead, L. M. "Policy Studies and Political Science." *Policy Studies Review* 5, no. 2 (1985): 319–35.

Meier, K. J., and D. R. Morgan. "Citizen Compliance with Public Policy: The National Maximum Speed Law." *The Western Political Quarterly* 35, no. 2 (June 1, 1982): 258–73.

Mergel, I. "Social Affordances of Agile Governance." *Public Administration Review* 84, no. 5 (2024): 932–47.

Mergel, I., S. Ganapati, and A. B. Whitford. "Agile: A New Way of Governing." *Public Administration Review* 81, no. 1 (2021): 161–65.

Migone, Andrea, and Michael Howlett. "Multiple Streams and Plausibility Cones: Using Concepts from Future Studies to Depict Policy Dynamics." *International Journal of Public Administration* (2025): 1–13. https://doi.org/10.1080/01900692.2024.2381769.

Migone, A., and M. Howlett. "Assessing the 'Forgotten Fundamental' in Policy Advisory Systems Research: Policy Shops and the Role(s) of Core Policy Professionals." *Australian Journal of Public Administration* 83, no. 2 (2024): 192–214.

Migone, A., M. R. McGregor, K. Brock, and M. Howlett. "Super-Users and Hyper-Experts in the Provision of Policy Advice: Evidence from a Survey of Canadian Academics." *European Policy Analysis* 8, no. 4 (2022): 370–93.

Milkman, K. L. "Unsure What the Future Will Bring? You May Overindulge: Uncertainty Increases the Appeal of Wants over Shoulds." *Organizational Behavior and Human Decision Processes* 119, no. 2 (2012): 163–76.

Mirowski, P. "Inherent Vice: Minsky, Markomata, and the Tendency of Markets to Undermine Themselves." *Journal of Institutional Economics* 6, no. 4 (December 2010): 415–43.

Moore, M. H. "Public Value Accounting: Establishing the Philosophical Basis." *Public Administration Review* 74, no. 4 (2014): 465–77.

Moore, M. H. "Public Value as the Focus of Strategy." *Australian Journal of Public Administration* 53, no. 3 (1994): 296–303.

Moore, M. H. *Creating Public Value: Strategic Management in Government*. Cambridge, MA: Harvard University Press, 1995.

Morgan, M. G., and M. Henrion. *Uncertainty: A Guide to Dealing with Uncertainty in Quantitative Risk and Policy Analysis*. Cambridge: Cambridge University Press, 1990.

Moss, D. A. *When All Else Fails: Government as the Ultimate Risk Manager*. Cambridge, MA: Harvard University Press, 2002.

Moxey, A., B. White, and A. Ozanne. (1999). "Efficient Contract Design for Agri-Environment Policy." *Journal of Agricultural Economics* 50, no. 2 (1999): 187–202.

Mueller, B. "Why Public Policies Fail: Policymaking under Complexity." *EconomiA* 21, no. 2 (2020): 311–23.

Mulford, C. L., and A. Etzioni. "Why They Don't Even When They Ought to: Implications of Compliance Theory for Policymakers." In A. Etzioni (Ed.), *Policy Research* (pp. 47–62). Leiden: E.J. Brill, 1978.

Mullainathan, S., and E. Shafir. *Scarcity: Why Having Too Little Means So Much*. New York: Picador, Henry Holt and Company, 2014.

Munn, N., 2014. "Capacity-Testing as a Means of Increasing Political Inclusion." *Democratization* 21, no. 6 (2014): 1134–52.

Nair, S., and M. Howlett "Policy Myopia as a Source of Policy Failure: Adaptation and Policy Learning under Deep Uncertainty." *Policy & Politics* 45, no. 1 (2017): 103–18.

National Audit Office. (2004). Managing Risks to Improve Public Services. London: National Audit Office. August 21, 2020. www.nao.org.uk/wp-content/uploads/2004/10/03041078.pdf.

Nilsen, Per. "Making Sense of Implementation Theories, Models and Frameworks." *Implementation Science* 10, no. 1 (April 21, 2015): 53–79.

NIST. Risk Management Framework for Information Systems and Organizations: A System Life Cycle Approach for Security and Privacy. SP 800-37 Rev. 2, 2018. January 23, 2022. https://csrc.nist.gov/publications/detail/sp/800-37/rev-2/final.

Norris, P., and R. Inglehart. *Cultural Backlash: Trump, Brexit, and Authoritarian Populism*. Cambridge: Cambridge University Press, 2019.

O'Flynn, J. "Rethinking Relationships: Clarity, Contingency, and Capabilities." *Policy Design and Practice* 2, no. 2 (April 3, 2019): 115–36.

Okonta, I. "'Biafra of the Mind': MASSOB and the Mobilization of History." In *Postcolonial Conflict and the Question of Genocide* (pp. 360–86). New York: Routledge, 2017.

Olsen, J. P., and B. G. Peters. *Lessons from Experience: Experiential Learning in Administrative Reforms in Eight Democracies*. Oslo: Scandinavian University Press, 1996.

Olsson, R. "Risk Management in a Multi-project Environment: An Approach to Manage Portfolio Risks." *International Journal of Quality & Reliability Management* 25 no. 1 (2008): 60–71.

Oreskes, N., and E. M. Conway. *Merchants of Doubt: How a Handful of Scientists Obscured the Truth on Issues from Tobacco Smoke to Global Warming*. Export ed. New York: Bloomsbury Press, 2011.

Pachanee, C. "Incoherent Policies on Universal Coverage of Health Insurance and Promotion of International Trade in Health Services in Thailand." *Health Policy and Planning* 21, no. 4 (2006): 310–18.

Painter, M., and J. Pierre, eds. *Challenges to State Policy Capacity: Global Trends and Comparative Perspectives*. London: Palgrave Macmillan, 2005.

Pal, L. A., J. Maxwell, and G. Lussier. *Assessing the Public Interest in the 21st Century: A Framework* (p. 4). Ottawa: Canadian Policy Research Networks, 2004.

Pandemic Prevention Institute. Ending the Current Covid-19 Pandemic and Preventing Future Global Disease Outbreaks Requires Fast, Accurate Data. The Rockefeller Foundation (blog), 2021. www.rockefellerfoundation.org/pandemicpreventioninstitute/.

Papacharissi, Z. *A Private Sphere: Democracy in a Digital Age*. Cambridge: Polity, 2010.

Parker, C. "Reducing the Risk of Policy Failure: Challenges for Regulatory Compliance." *OECD*. 8, no. 77 (2000): 1–91.

Parkhurst, J. O. "Appeals to Evidence for the Resolution of Wicked Problems: The Origins and Mechanisms of Evidentiary Bias." *Policy Sciences* 49, no. 4 (2016): 373–93.

Pawson, P. "Evidence-based Policy: In Search of a Method." *Evaluation* 8, no. 2 (2002): 157–81.

Pellegrinelli, S. "Programme Management: Organising Project-Based Change." *International Journal of Project Management* 15 no. 3 (1997): 141–49.

Pérez-Morote, R., H. Nuno Rito Ribeiro, J. Calleja-Lozano, and Jesús F. Santos-Peñalver. "Risk and Conditioning Factors in the Public Internal Control. Weaknesses in Public Management Concerning the Procurement of Expenditure Files." *Public Money & Management* forthcoming (2024): 1–11.

Perl, A., M. Howlett, and M. Ramesh. "Policy-Making and Truthiness: Can Existing Policy Models Cope with Politicized Evidence and Willful Ignorance in a 'Post-Fact' World?" *Policy Sciences* 51, no. 4 (December 2018): 581–600.

Persson, J., and L. Mathiassen. "A Process for Managing Risks in Distributed Teams." IEEE Software 27, no. 1 (2009): 20–29.

Peters, B. Guy, and Maximilian L Nagel. "From Benign to Malign: Unintended Consequences and the Growth of Zombie Policies." *Policy and Society*, 2025. https://doi.org/10.1093/polsoc/puae039.

Peters, B. Guy, P. Ravinet, M. Howlett, et al. *Designing for Policy Effectiveness: Defining and Understanding a Concept*. Elements Series. Cambridge: Cambridge University Press, 2018.

Pickering, S., and C. Lambert, C. "Deterrence: Australia's Refugee Policy." *Current Issues in Criminal Justice* 14, no. 1 (2002): 65–86.

Pierson, P. "'Policy Feedbacks' and Political Change: Contrasting Reagan and Thatcher's Pension Reform Initiatives." *Studies in American Political Development* 6 (1992), 359–90.

Pierson, P. "When Effect Becomes Cause: Policy Feedback and Political Change." *World Politics* 45, no. 4 (1993): 595–628.

Plaček, M., M. Půček, and F. Ochrana. "Identifying Corruption Risk: A Comparison of Bulgaria and the Czech Republic." *Journal of Comparative Policy Analysis: Research and Practice* 21, no. 4 (2018): 366–84.

Plehwe, D., and K. Günaydin. "Whither Energiewende? Strategies to Manufacture Uncertainty and Unknowing to Redirect Germany's Renewable Energy Law." *International Journal of Public Policy* 16, no. 5–6 (2022): 270–92.

Prime Minister's Strategy Unit. Risk: Improving Government's Capability to Handle Risk and Uncertainty. London: UK Cabinet Office, 2002. August 23, 2020, www.integra.com.bo/articulos/RISK%20IMPROVING%20 GOVERMENT.pdf.

Profeti, Stefania, and Federico Toth. "Leading Targets to Comply. Uncertainty Issues in the Design of 'Intrinsic Motivation-Driven Policies.'" *Policy Design and Practice* (2025): 1–15. https://doi.org/10.1080/25741292.2025.2466297.

Project Management Institute. The Standard for Portfolio Management – Second Edition, 2nd ed. Project Management Institute, Newtown Square, PA, 2008.

Pwc. (n.d.) Risk Management and Compliance. Risk Assurance. Services. www .pwc.com/me/en/services/risk-assurance/risk-management-and-compliance .html.

Quah, Jon T. S. "Anti-Corruption Agencies in Four Asian Countries: A Comparative Analysis." *International Public Management Review* 8, no. 2 (2007): 73–96.

Radin, B. A. *Beyond Machiavelli: Policy Analysis Comes of Age*. Washington, DC: Georgetown University Press, 2000.

Renn, O. *Risk Governance: Coping with Uncertainty in a Complex World*. (R. E. Löfstedt, Ed.) London: EarthScan, 2008.

Rietig, K. "Learning in the European Commission's Renewable Energy Policy-Making and Climate Governance." In C. A. Dunlop, C. M. Radaelli, and P. Trein (Eds.), *Learning in Public Policy: Analysis, Modes and Outcomes* (pp. 51–74), International Series on Public Policy. Cham: Springer International, 2018.

Rietig, K. "Leveraging the Power of Learning to Overcome Negotiation Deadlocks in Global Climate Governance and Low Carbon Transitions." *Journal of Environmental Policy & Planning* 21, no. 3 (2019): 228–41.

Rittel, H. W. J., and M. M. Webber. "Dilemmas in a General Theory of Planning." *Policy Sciences* 4, no. 2 (1973): 155–69.

Rodda, W. H. *Inland Marine and Transportation Insurance*. Englewood Cliffs: Prentice Hall, 1949.

Rogge, K. S., and K. Reichardt. "Policy Mixes for Sustainability Transitions: An Extended Concept and Framework for Analysis." *Research Policy* 45, no. 8 (October 2016): 1620–35.

Roth, K. "The Dangerous Rise of Populism: Global Attacks on Human Rights Values." *Journal of International Affairs* 79, no. 4 (2017), 79–84.

Rummel, R. J. *Power Kills: Democracy as a Method of Nonviolence*. New York: Routledge, 2017.

Rupprecht, A. "'Inherent Vice': Marine Insurance, Slave Ship Rebellion and the Law." *Race & Class* 57, no. 3 (January 1, 2016): 31–44.

Sager, F., and Y. Rielle. "Sorting through the Garbage Can: Under What Conditions Do Governments Adopt Policy Programs?" *Policy Sciences* 46, no. 1 (March 1, 2013): 1–21.

Salamon, L. M. *The Tools of Government: A Guide to the New Governance.* New York: Oxford University Press, 2002.

Sanchez, H., B. Robert, and R. Pellerin. "A Project Portfolio Risk-Opportunity Identification Framework." *Project Management Journal* 39, no. 3 (2008): 97–109.

Sanchez, H., B. Robert, M. Bourgault, and R. Pellerin. "Risk Management Applied to Projects, Programs, and Portfolios." *International Journal of Managing Projects in Business*, 2, no. 1 (2009): 14–35.

Sanderson, I. "Evaluation in Complex Policy Systems." *Evaluation* 6, no. 4 (2000): 433–54.

Sanderson, I. "Intelligent Policy Making for a Complex World: Pragmatism, Evidence and Learning." *Political Studies* 57, no. 4 (2009): 699–719.

Saward, M. *Co-Optive Politics and State Legitimacy.* Aldershot: Dartmouth, 1992.

Scharpf, F. W. *Governing in Europe. Effective and Democratic?* Oxford: Oxford University Press, 1999.

Scharpf, F. W. "Problem-solving Effectiveness and Democratic Accountability in the EU." (Working Paper 03/1, Max Planck Institute for the Study of Societies, February 2003).

Schnell, S. "To Know Is to Act? Revisiting the Impact of Government Transparency on Corruption." *Public Administration and Development* 43, no. 5 (2023): 355–67.

Schneider, A., and H. Ingram. "Behavioral Assumptions of Policy Tools." *The Journal of Politics* 52, no. 2 (1990a): 510–29.

Schneider, A. L., and H. Ingram. "Policy Design: Elements, Premises and Strategies." In S. S. Nagel (Ed.), *Policy Theory and Policy Evaluation: Concepts, Knowledge, Causes and Norms*, (pp. 77–102). New York: Greenwood, 1990b.

Schneider, A., and H. Ingram. "Social Construction of Target Populations: Implications for Politics and Policy." *American Political Science Review* 87, no. 2 (1993): 334–47.

Schneider, A. L., and H. M. Ingram, eds. *Deserving and Entitled: Social Constructions and Public Policy.* SUNY Series in Public Policy. Albany: State University of New York, 2005.

Scholz, J. T. "Cooperative Regulatory Enforcement and the Politics of Administrative Effectiveness." *American Political Science Review* 85, no. 1 (1991): 115–36.

Shafir, E., ed. *The Behavioral Foundations of Public Policy*. Princeton: Princeton University Press, 2013.

Shore, C., S. Wright, and D. Pero, eds. *Policy Worlds: Anthropology and Analysis of Contemporary Power*. New York: Berghahn Books, 2011.

Sidney, M. S. "Policy Formulation: Design and Tools." In F. Fischer, G. J. Miller, and M. S. Sidney (Eds.), *Handbook of Public Policy Analysis: Theory, Politics and Methods* (pp. 79–87). New Brunswick: CRC Taylor & Francis, 2007.

Simon, H. "The Logic of Heuristic Decision Making." In N. Rescher (Ed.), *The Logic of Decision and Action* (pp. 1–35). Pittsburgh: University of Pittsburgh Press, 1967.

Simon, H. A. "Rationality as Process and as Product of Thought." *The American Economic Review* 68, no. 2 (May 1, 1978): 1–16.

Simon, H. A. "The Structure of Ill Structured Problems." *Artificial Intelligence* 4, no. 3–4 (Winter 1973): 181–201.

Smith, G., and C. Wales. "Citizens' Juries and Deliberative Democracy." *Political Studies* 48, no. 1 (March 1, 2000): 51–65.

Solesbury, W. "The Ascendancy of Evidence." *Planning Theory and Practice* 3, no. 1 (2002): 90–96.

Somerville, W., and S. W. Goodman. "The Role of Networks in the Development of UK Migration Policy." *Political Studies* 58, no. 5 (2010): 951–70.

Sørensen, E., and J. Torfing. "Network Governance and Post-liberal Democracy." *Administrative Theory & Praxis* 27, no. 2 (2005): 197–237.

Spash, C. L., and A. Y. Lo. "Australia's Carbon Tax: A Sheep in Wolf's Clothing?" *The Economic and Labour Relations Review* 23, no. 1 (2012): 67–86.

St. Denny, E., and P. Zittoun, eds. *Handbook of Teaching Public Policy*. First. Handbooks of Research on Public Policy. Northampton: Edward Elgar, 2024.

Stark, A., and S. Yates. *Public Inquiries and Policy Design*. Cambridge: Cambridge University Press, 2024.

Stark, A., and S. Yates. "Public Inquiries as Procedural Policy Tools." *Policy and Society* 40, no. 3 (July 19, 2021): 345–61.

Stokey, E., and R. Zeckhauser. *A Primer for Policy Analysis*. New York: W.W. Norton, 1978.

Sullivan, T. A. "Coming to Our Census: How Social Statistics Underpin Our Democracy (and Republic)." *Harvard Data Science Review* 2, no. 1 (2020): n.p.

Taylor, C. M., E. A. Gallagher, S. J. T. Pollard, et al. "Environmental Regulation in Transition: Policy Officials' Views of Regulatory Instruments and Their Mapping to Environmental Risks." *Science of the Total Environment* 646 (2019): 811–20.

Taylor, C., S. Pollard, S. Rocks, and A. Angus. "Selecting Policy Instruments for Better Environmental Regulation: A Critique and Future Research Agenda." *Environmental Policy and Governance* 22 (2012): 268–92.

Taylor, J. "Public Officials' Gaming of Performance Measures and Targets: The Nexus between Motivation and Opportunity." *Public Performance & Management Review* 44, no. 2 (March 4, 2021): 272–93.

Taylor, J., J. McDonnell, and H. Duong. "Bureaucratic Gaming: Causes and Consequences for Policy-Making." *International Journal of Public Policy* 16, no. 5–6 (2022): 253–69.

Tazreiter C. "Dignity and the Invisible Spaces of Irregular Migration: Rendering Asylum Seekers Invisible through Off-Shore Detention." In E. Sieh, J. McGregor (Eds.) *Human Dignity*. London: Palgrave Macmillan, 2017a

Tazreiter, C. "The Unlucky in the 'Lucky Country': Asylum Seekers, Irregular Migrants and Refugees and Australia's Politics of Disappearance." *Australian Journal of Human Rights* 23, no. 2 (2017b): 242–60.

Teller, J., and A. Kock. "An Empirical Investigation on How Portfolio Risk Management Influences Project Portfolio Success." *International Journal of Project Management* 31 (2013): 817–29.

Teo, A. K. J., R. Kay Jin Tan, and K. Prem. "Concealment of Potential Exposure to COVID-19 and Its Impact on Outbreak Control: Lessons from the HIV Response." *The American Journal of Tropical Medicine and Hygiene* 103, no. 1 (2020): 35–37.

Thaler, R. H. "From Cashews to Nudges: The Evolution of Behavioral Economics." *American Economic Review* 108, no. 6 (2018): 1265–87.

Thaler, Richard H., Cass R. Sunstein, and John P. Balz. "Choice Architecture." SSRN Scholarly Paper. Rochester, NY: Social Science Research Network, April 2, 2010. http://papers.ssrn.com/abstract=1583509.

Thomas, A. S., T. L. Milfont, and M. C. Gavin. "A New Approach to Identifying the Drivers of Regulation Compliance Using Multivariate Behavioural Models." Edited by Petr Heneberg. *PLOS ONE* 11, no. 10 (October 11, 2016): e0163868.

Torgerson, D. *The Policy Sciences of Harold Lasswell: Contextual Orientation and the Critical Dimension*. Northampton: Edward Elgar, 2024.

Tribe, L. H. "Policy Science: Analysis or Ideology?" *Philosophy and Public Affairs* 2, no. 1 (1972): 66–110.

Turnbull, N. "Policy Design: Its Enduring Appeal in a Complex World and How to Think It Differently." *Public Policy and Administration* 33, no. 4 (2018): 357–64.

Uribe, C. A. "The Dark Side of Social Capital Re-Examined from a Policy Analysis Perspective: Networks of Trust and Corruption." *Journal of Comparative Policy Analysis: Research and Practice* 16, no. 2 (March 15, 2014): 175–89.

References

United Nations Human Rights Council. *Impact of Measures to Address Terrorism and Violent Extremism on Civic Space and the Rights of Civil Society Actors and Human Rights Defenders: Report of the Special Rapporteur on the Promotion and Protection of Human Rights and Fundamental Freedoms While Countering Terrorism (A/HRC/40/52)*. United Nations, 2019. https://digitallibrary.un.org/record/3802009.

United Nations Special Rapporteur. *Promotion and Protection of the Right to Freedom of Opinion and Expression*. United Nations General Assembly, A/74/486, 2019.

Van Buuren, A., J. M. Lewis, and B. Guy Peters, eds. *Policy-Making as Designing: The Added Value of Design Thinking for Public Administration and Public Policy*. Bristol: Policy Press, 2023.

Van der Sluijs, J. "Uncertainty as a Monster in the Science-Policy Interface: Four Coping Strategies." *Water Science and Technology: A Journal of the International Association on Water Pollution Research* 52, no. 6 (2005): 87–92.

Van der Steen, M. A., and M. J. W. Van Twist. "Foresight and Long-Term Policy-Making: An Analysis of Anticipatory Boundary Work in Policy Organizations in The Netherlands." *Futures* 54 (2013): 33–42.

Vargas Cullell, J. "Democracy and the Quality of Democracy: Empirical Findings and Methodological and Theoretical Issues Drawn from the Citizen Audit of the Quality of Democracy in Costa Rica." In G. O'Donnell, J. Vargas Cullell, and O. M. Iazzetta (Eds.), *The Quality of Democracy: Theory and Applications* (pp. 47–99). Notre Dame, IN: University of Notre Dame Press, 2004

Vine, E., and J. Sathaye. "The Monitoring, Evaluation, Reporting and Verification of Climate Change Projects." *Mitigation and Adaptation Strategies for Global Change* 4, no. 1 (1999): 43–60.

Viscusi, W. K., and T. Gayer. "Behavioral Public Choice: The Behavioral Paradox of Government Policy." *Harvard Journal of Law & Public Policy* 38, no. 3 (2015): 973–1009.

Wagle, U. "The Policy Science of Democracy: The Issues of Methodology and Citizen Participation." *Policy Sciences* 33, no. 2 (2000): 207–223.

Walker, W. E., M. Haasnoot, and J. H. Kwakkel. "Review: Adapt or Perish: A Review of Planning Approaches for Adaptation under Deep Uncertainty." *Sustainability* 5 (2013): 955–79.

Weaver, K. *"But Will It Work?: Implementation Analysis to Improve Government Performance."* Washington, DC: Brookings Institution, 2010.

Weaver, R. K. Target Compliance: The Final Frontier of Policy Implementation. Governance Studies at Brookings, 2009.

Weaver, R. K. "Compliance Regimes and Barriers to Behavioral Change: Compliance Regimes and Behavioral Change." *Governance* 27, no. 2 (April 2014): 243–65.

Weaver, R. K. "Getting People to Behave: Research Lessons for Policy Makers." *Public Administration Review* 75, no. 6 (2015): 806–16.

Weaver, R. K. *Policy Leadership and the Blame Trap: Seven Strategies for Avoiding Policy Stalemate.* Governance Studies. Brookings Institution, 2013.

Webster, M. "Communicating Climate Change Uncertainty to Policy–Makers and the Public." *Climatic Change* 61, no. 1–2 (2003): 1–8.

Weinberg, L., 1991. "Turning to Terror: The Conditions under Which Political Parties Turn to Terrorist Activities." *Comparative Politics* 23, no. 4 (1991): 423–38.

Wheeler, C. "The Public Interest: We Know It's Important, but Do We Know What It Means?" In *AIAL Forum*, no. 48 (April 2006): 12–25.

Whiteford, P. (2021). "Debt by Design: The Anatomy of a Social Policy Fiasco– Or was It Something Worse? *Australian Journal of Public Administration* 80 (2021): 340–60.

Wholey, J. S., H. P. Hatry, and K. E. Newcomer. *Handbook of Practical Program Evaluation.* 3rd ed. San Francisco: Jossey-Bass, 2010.

Wilson, W. "The Study of Administration." *Political Science Quarterly* 2, no. 2 (1887): 197–222.

Wintrobe, R. "Some Lessons on the Efficiency of Democracy from a Study of Dictatorship." In *The Political Dimension of Economic Growth: Proceedings of the IEA Conference held in San José, Costa Rica* (pp. 20–37). London: Palgrave Macmillan UK, April 1998.

Wintrobe, R. *The Political Economy of Dictatorship.* Cambridge: Cambridge University Press, 2000.

Wu, X., M. Ramesh, and M. Howlett. "Policy Capacity: A Conceptual Framework for Understanding Policy Competences and Capabilities." *Policy and Society* 34, no. 3–4 (2015): 165–71.

Wu, X., M. Ramesh, M. Howlett, and S. A. Fritzen. *The Public Policy Primer: Managing the Policy Process.* 2nd ed. London: Routledge, 2017.

Yackee, J. W., and S. W. Yackee. "Administrative Procedures and Bureaucratic Performance: Is Federal Rule-Making 'Ossified'?" *Journal of Public Administration Research and Theory* 20, no. 2 (April 1, 2010): 261–82.

Zakaria, F. *The Future of Freedom: Illiberal Democracy at Home and Abroad.* Revised Edition. New York: W.W. Norton & Company, 2007.

Zaret, D. *Origins of Democratic Culture: Printing, Petitions, and the Public Sphere in Early-Modern England.* Princeton, N.J.: Princeton University Press, 2000.

About the Authors

Michael Howlett is the Burnaby Mountain Professor and Canada Research Chair (Tier 1) in the Department of Political Science at Simon Fraser University in Burnaby, British Columbia, and was Yong Pung How Chair Professor in the Lee Kuan Yew School of Public Policy at the National University of Singapore. He has been Visiting Professor at the University of Cagliari, and the Hong Kong University of Science and Technology and has published leading textbooks and articles on topics related to Canadian politics, natural resource and environmental policy, Canadian public policy, public policy-making and policy instruments and design, among others. He has also served as co-editor of the Canadian Journal of Political Science and is currently editor-in-chief of Policy Sciences, as well as co-editor of the Journal of Comparative Policy Analysis, Policy & Society, and Policy Design and Practice. His current work deals with aspects of policy formulation and policy design, including the study of policy tools and instruments as well as formulation processes more generally.

Tim Legrand is Associate Professor of International Security at the University of Adelaide. His research is concerned with national and international dimensions of global security decision-making, particularly in transnational networks and institutions. His work traverses a range of themes, principally in global policy; blacklisting and sanctions, digital security, terrorism, political violence, and political exclusion. This research draws widely from critical scholarship in security studies to illuminate how threats are constructed and conceived, and how security policies are developed and deployed. Tim is author or editor of five books and more than fifty journal articles and chapters on terrorism, counter-terrorism, and national security policy-making, including most recently *Banning Them, Securing Us? Terrorism, Parliament and the Ritual of Proscription* (Manchester University Press, 2021) and *The Architecture of Policy Transfer* (Palgrave Macmillan, 2021). He has been co-editor of the *Australian Journal of International Affairs* since 2023.

Leong Ching is Vice Provost (Student Life) and Associate Professor at the Lee Kuan Yee School of Public Policy at the National University of Singapore (NUS). Her interests are motivated by theories of institutional change, including the role of economic and non-economic incentives. Her works include water policies, environmental behavior, public sector reform, and public narratives. Dr. Leong's current projects include experiments to test honesty in public behavior, large-scale field experiments on vaccine hesitancy, and trade-offs between self-interest and public environmental goods. She researches Asian countries and cities including China, Jakarta, and Manila, in addition to Singapore. She is on the editorial boards of Policy Sciences, Water, and the International Journal of Water Resources and Development.

Cambridge Elements

Public Policy

M. Ramesh
National University of Singapore (NUS)
M. Ramesh is UNESCO Chair on Social Policy Design at the Lee Kuan Yew School of Public Policy, NUS. His research focuses on governance and social policy in East and Southeast Asia, in addition to public policy institutions and processes. He has published extensively in reputed international journals. He is co-editor of *Policy and Society* and *Policy Design and Practice*.

Michael Howlett
Simon Fraser University, British Columbia
Michael Howlett is Burnaby Mountain Professor and Canada Research Chair (Tier1) in the Department of Political Science, Simon Fraser University. He specialises in public policy analysis, and resource and environmental policy. He is currently editor-in-chief of *Policy Sciences* and co-editor of the *Journal of Comparative Policy Analysis, Policy and Society* and *Policy Design and Practice*.

Xun WU
Hong Kong University of Science and Technology (Guangzhou)
Xun WU is currently a Professor at the Innovation, Policy and Entrepreneurship Thrust at the Society Hub of Hong Kong University of Science and Technology (Guangzhou). He is a policy scientist with a strong interest in the linkage between policy analysis and public management. Trained in engineering, economics, public administration, and policy analysis, his research seeks to make contribution to the design of effective public policies in dealing emerging policy challenges across Asian countries.

Judith Clifton
University of Cantabria
Judith Clifton is Professor of Economics at the University of Cantabria, Spain, and Editor-in-Chief of *Journal of Economic Policy Reform*. Her research interests include the determinants and consequences of public policy across a wide range of public services, from infrastructure to health, particularly in Europe and Latin America, as well as public banks, especially, the European Investment Bank. Most recently, she is principal investigator on the Horizon Europe Project GREENPATHS (www.greenpaths.info) on the just green transition.

Eduardo Araral
National University of Singapore (NUS)
Eduardo Araral specializes in the study of the causes and consequences of institutions for collective action and the governance of the commons. He is widely published in various journals and books and has presented in more than ninety conferences. Ed was a 2021–22 Fellow at the Center for Advanced Study of Behavioral Sciences, Stanford University. He has received more than US$6.6 million in external research grants as the lead or co-PI for public agencies and corporations. He currently serves as a Special Issue Editor (collective action, commons, institutions, governance) for World Development and is a member of the editorial boards of *Water Economics and Policy*, *World Development Sustainability*, *Water Alternatives* and the *International Journal of the Commons*.

About the Series

Elements in Public Policy is a concise and authoritative collection of assessments of the state of the art and future research directions in public policy research, as well as substantive new research on key topics. Edited by leading scholars in the field, the series is an ideal medium for reflecting on and advancing the understanding of critical issues in the public sphere. Collectively, the series provides a forum for broad and diverse coverage of all major topics in the field while integrating different disciplinary and methodological approaches.

Cambridge Elements

Public Policy

Elements in the Series

Policy Feedback: How Policies Shape Politics
Daniel Béland, Andrea Louise Campbell and R. Kent Weaver

Government Transparency: State of the Art and New Perspectives
Gregory Porumbescu, Albert Meijer and Stephan Grimmelikhuijsen

Relationality: The Inner Life of Public Policy
Raul P. Lejano and Wing Shan Kan

Understanding Accountability in Democratic Governance
Yannis Papadopoulos

Public Inquiries and Policy Design
Alastair Stark and Sophie Yates

Multiple Streams and Policy Ambiguity
Rob A. DeLeo, Reimut Zohlnhöfer and Nikolaos Zahariadis

Designing Behavioural Insights for Policy: Processes, Capacities & Institutions
Ishani Mukherjee and Assel Mussagulova

Robust Governance in Turbulent Times
Christopher Ansell, Eva Sørensen, Jacob Torfing and Jarle Trondal

Public Contracting for Social Outcomes
Clare J FitzGerald and Ruairi Macdonald

Policy Entrepreneurs, Crises, and Policy Change
Evangelia Petridou, Jörgen Sparf, Nikolaos Zahariadis and Thomas Birkland

Symbolic Policy
Laurie Boussaguet and Florence Faucher

Bad Public Policy: Malignity, Volatility, and the Inherent Vices of Policy-Making
Michael Howlett, Ching Leong and Tim Legrand

A full series listing is available at: www.cambridge.org/EPPO

For EU product safety concerns, contact us at Calle de José Abascal, 56–1°,
28003 Madrid, Spain or eugpsr@cambridge.org.

www.ingramcontent.com/pod-product-compliance
Lightning Source LLC
LaVergne TN
LVHW020349260326
834688LV00045B/1615